Richard Wagner

Das Rheingold

(The Rhinegold)

OPERA STUDY GUIDE

WITH

LIBRETTO

OPERA CLASSICS LIBRARY™SERIES

Edited by Burton D. Fisher
Principal lecturer, *Opera Journeys Lecture Series*

Opera Journeys™ Publishing   /   Boca Raton, Florida

WEBSITE: www.operajourneys.com   E MAIL: operaj@bellsouth.net

Contents

a Prelude....   Page 7

Das Rheingold (Provenance)   Page 9

A Wagner Biography   Page 11

Wagner's Ring and the Conquest of Will   Page 15

A Prologue to the PROLOGUE   Page 23

Principal Characters in *Das Rheingold*   Page 25

Das Rheingold Synopsis and Overview   Page 27

Story Narrative with Music Highlight Examples   Page 31

Libretto with Music Highlight Examples   Page 47

               Prologue and Scene 1   Page 49

               Scene 2   Page 60

               Scene 3   Page 75

               Scene 4   Page 85

Dictionary of Opera and Musical Terms   Page 101

Opera Journeys' "Flagship" Publications   Page 111

Opera Journeys™ *Mini Guide Series*

Opera Classics Library™ *Series*

Opera Journeys™ *Libretto Series*

A History of Opera:
Milestones and Metamorphoses

Mozart's Da Ponte Operas

PUCCINI COMPANION

Verdi Companion: 27 Opera Study Guide

Over 125 GUIDES & LIBRETTI AVAILABLE: Print or Ebook

•The Abduction from the Seraglio •Adriana Lecouvreur •L'Africaine •Aida
•Andrea Chénier •Anna Bolena •Ariadne auf Naxos •Armida •Attila
•The Ballad of Baby Doe •The Barber of Seville •Duke Bluebeard's Castle
•La Bohème •Boris Godunov •Candide •Capriccio •Carmen
•Cavalleria Rusticana •Cendrillon •La Cenerentola •La Clemenza di Tito
•Le Comte Ory •Così fan tutte •The Crucible •La Damnation de Faust
•The Death of Klinghoffer •Doctor Atomic •Don Carlo •Don Giovanni
•Don Pasquale •La Donna del Lago •The Elixir of Love •Elektra •Ernani
•Eugene Onegin •Exploring Wagner's Ring •Falstaff •La Fanciulla del West
•Faust •La Fille du Régiment •Fidelio •Die Fledermaus •The Flying Dutchman
•Die Frau ohne Schatten •Der Freischütz •Gianni Schicchi •La Gioconda
•Hamlet •Hansel and Gretel •Henry VIII •Iolanta •L'Italiana in Algeri
•Les Huguenots •Iphigénie en Tauride •Julius Caesar •Lakmé •Lohengrin
•Lucia di Lammermoor •Macbeth •Madama Butterfly •The Magic Flute
•The Makropolis Case •Manon •Manon Lescaut •Maria Stuarda
•The Marriage of Figaro •A Masked Ball •Die Meistersinger •The Mikado
•Nabucco •Nixon in China •Norma •Of Mice and Men •Orfeo ed Euridice
•Otello •I Pagliacci •Parsifal •The Pearl Fishers •Pelléas et Mélisande
•Porgy and Bess •Prince Igor •I Puritani •The Queen of Spades
•The Rake's Progress •The Rape of Lucretia •The Rhinegold •Rigoletto
•The Ring of the Nibelung •Roberto Devereaux •Rodalinda •Roméo et Juliette
•La Rondine •Der Rosenkavalier •Rusalka •Salome •Samson and Delilah
•Show Boat •Siegfried •Simon Boccanegra •La Sonnambula •Suor Angelica
•Susannah •Il Tabarro •The Tales of Hoffmann •Tannhäuser •Thaïs •Tosca
•La Traviata •Tristan and Isolde •Il Trittico •Les Troyens •Il Trovatore
•Turandot •The Valkyrie •Werther •West Side Story •Wozzeck

WWW.OPERAJOURNEYS.COM

a *Prelude........*

OPERA CLASSICS LIBRARY's

Das Rheingold

STUDY GUIDE WITH LIBRETTO

Das Rheingold (The Rhinegold) is the first opera of Wagner's colossal music drama, *Der Ring des Nibelungen* (The Ring of the Nibelung).

Das Rheingold begins at the moment of creation: it is the beginning of the world when a primordial wasteland of surging waters evolve into a brutal struggle for power between Gods, Giants, and Dwarfs.

The eternal battle continues in the three subsequent operas of the *Ring*: *Die Walküre* (The Valkyrie); *Siegfried; Götterdämmerung* (Twilight of the Gods).

OPERA CLASSICS LIBRARY explores the greatness of Wagner's *Das Rheingold,* which includes *A Wagner Biography*; the *Conquest of Will,* which explores Wagner's inspiration to musically dramatize the saga; a *Prologue to the PROLOGUE*; and a *Story Synopsis and Overview* with music highlight examples.

The new *Libretto* provides the German-English translation in a side-by-side format. In addition, the text includes a *Dictionary of Opera and Musical Terms.*

The opera art form is the sum of many artistic expressions: theatrical drama, music, scenery, poetry, dance, acting and gesture. In opera, the music composer is the dramatist; he applies the emotive power of his music with the kinetic intensity of the prose to provide powerful theater, an impact on one's sensibilities that can reach into the very depths of the human soul.

Burton D. Fisher
Editor
OPERA CLASSICS LIBRARY

Das Rheingold
(THE RHINEGOLD)

Music drama with a Prelude and four scenes

Music
by
Richard Wagner

Drama written
by
Richard Wagner

Premiere: Hoftheater in Munich, 1869

Das Rheingold **is the first music drama, or** *Prologue*
to *Der Ring des Nibelungen* **(The Ring of the Nibelng)**

A Wagner Biography

Richard Wagner (1813 — 1883) was born in Leipzig, Germany; he became one of the world's most important, influential and controversial figures in nineteenth-century music.

As a young boy, Wagner attended school in Dresden, Germany. He did not show aptitude in music and, in fact, his teacher said that he would most likely torture the piano in a most abominable fashion. But he was ambitious from a young age. When he was 11 years old, he wrote his first drama; by age 16, he was writing musical compositions.

In the obituary of the famous composer, the New York Times would later write, "In the face of mortifying failures and discouragements, he apparently never lost confidence in himself."

During Wagner's first creative period, 1839 — 1850, his opera style was fundamentally subservient to existing operatic traditions and conventions: he faithfully composed in the German Romantic style of Carl Maria von Weber (*Die Freischütz*), Giacomo Meyerbeer's grandiose French style (*Le Prophète, L'Africaine, Robert le Diable, Les Huguenots*), and the Italian bel canto style. The operatic architecture within those genres was primarily concerned with effects, atmosphere, characterization, and actions and climaxes, all presented with formal arias and ensemble numbers, choruses, scenes of pageantry, and ballet.

Wagner's operas from this early period were: *Die Feen* ("The Fairies"), based on Carlo Gozzi's *La Donna Serpente* ("The Serpent Woman"), an opera that was never performed during the composer's lifetime but premiered in 1888, five years after the composer's death; *Das Liebesverbot* ("The Ban on Love") (1836), a fiasco based on Shakespeare's *Measure for Measure; Rienzi, Der Letze Der Tribunen* ("Rienzi, Last of the Tribunes") (1842), a resounding success that was based on a Bulwer-Lytton novel; *Der Fliegende Holländer,* ("The Flying Dutchman") (1843); *Tannhäuser und der Sängerkrieg auf Wartburg* (1845) ("Tannhäuser and the Contest of Singers on the Wartburg"; and *Lohengrin* (1850), "the grand opera of all grand operas" that Franz Liszt deemed a Romantic masterpiece: "With *Lohengrin,* the old world of opera comes to an end."

During Wagner's second period, 1850 — 1882, he composed *The Ring of the Nibelung, Tristan und Isolde, Die Meistersinger,* and *Parsifal.* In those later works, Wagner incorporated revolutionary theories about opera — a new form of lyric theater called "music drama."

In 1839, at the age of 26, Wagner was an opera conductor at a small, provincial opera company in Riga, Latvia, the country at the time ruled by Russia. In a very short time, he was summarily dismissed, his rambunctious conducting style provoking disfavor, and his heavy debts becoming scandalous — to avoid creditors and debtors' prison, Wagner fled to Paris, the center of the European opera world.

Wagner arrived in Paris with the lofty ambition to become its brightest star, imagining fame and wealth. He appeared with letters of introduction to the "king" of opera, Giacomo Meyerbeer, and his yet uncompleted score for *Rienzi.*

During Wagner's three years in Paris — from 1839 to 1842 — he experienced agonizing hardships: he lived in penury and misery, and survived mostly by editing, writing, and performing musical "slave work" by transcribing operas for Jacques Halévy. The leading lights of French opera were Meyerbeer and Halévy, but Wagner was unsuccessful in securing their help and influence in having *Rienzi* produced at the Paris Opéra. He turned to despair: he became lonely and alienated, frustrated by his failures, and deeply bitter. His dreams were shattered, and his Paris years became a hopeless adventure, the non-French speaking Wagner considered himself an outsider.

Nevertheless, during the Parisian years, he completed both *Rienzi* and *Der Fliegende Hollander,* an incredible accomplishment since both operas possess extremely diverse stories and musical styles. *Rienzi* was a melodrama composed in the Italian bel canto style: it portrays the tribulations of its protagonist in conflict with power politics. *Dutchman* was composed in a unified, musically integrated style: it recounts the legend of a sailor doomed to travel the seas until he is redeemed by a woman's faithful love.

In 1842, the omnipotent Meyerbeer, changed the young composer's fortunes by using his influence to persuade the Dresden opera to produce *Rienzi;* the opera became an outstanding success, actually, the most successful opera during Wagner's lifetime. Although it is frequently revived in the contemporary repertory, it has become overshadowed by Wagner's later works.

Nevertheless, *Rienzi* catapulted Wagner to operatic stardom, prompting the Royal Saxon Court Theater in Dresden to appoint him Kapellmeister — the year was 1843, and Wagner was twenty-nine-years-old. That same year, *Dutchman* was mounted at Dresden to a rather mediocre reception; it was followed by *Tannhäuser* (1845), and *Lohengrin,* introduced by Franz Liszt at Weimar in 1850.

During the second half of the 19th century, Richard Wagner revolutionized opera with his conceptions of music drama: he created a seamless continuity between opera's internal architectural elements by virtually eliminating the formal structures of recitative and aria (or set piece); the result became a seamless continuity of music and text in the evolving drama. Through leading motives, or leitmotifs, the orchestra exposed the thoughts and ideas of the characters, but the orchestra was now transformed from accompanist into a symphonic unit; it became an integral protagonist of the drama that provided "endliche melodie," or an endless chain of music.

Wagner's *Tristan and Isolde* is vast in its concept and design, bold in its execution, revolutionary in its operatic structure, and exacting in its demands on singers and the orchestra. In this opera, Wagner's music-drama esthetics were first materialized: the extensive use of leitmotifs, the integration of the orchestra into the drama, and the dramatic unity of all its artistic elements.

The leitmotif of the entire music drama is the exaltation of love: as Wagner commented, "a monument to this loveliest of all dreams." In this opera, Wagner spiritualized love: an ideal beyond experienced emotions or the material world that is consummated metaphysically, or as a transcendent experience.

Musically, *Tristan and Isolde* represents a milestone — if not a revolution — in the history of music: its music emancipated dissonance from tonality and set the stage for future harmonic adventurism; the music score of *Tristan and Isolde* has been deemed the beginning of modern music, Wagner's harmonic innovations continuing into modern times. The score is dominated by discords, an innovation that broke all the existing rules of tonality: for hundreds of years before *Tristan and Isolde*, the essence of music was tonality; all music was composed in keys, chords could be identified with keys, or identified as transitional chords between keys.

The "Tristan Chord" — f, b, d sharp, g sharp, appearing initially in the second full measure of the Prelude and associated with Grief or Sorrow — is perhaps the most famous chord in the history of music, its essence challenging conventional analysis. The Tristan Chord is a discord; it partially resolves and it is partially suspended, creating a sense of both resolution and dissonance. As the music progresses new discords are created: the result is that the ear becomes partially satisfied by the resolution, but dissatisfied by the suspension; a lack of resolution that creates a sense of tension as the listener consciously and unconsciously craves for resolution. Wagner built the harmonics of the entire opera on discord and lack of resolution, except the final chord, its resolution suggesting a finality: the culmination of insatiable yearning.

Tristan and Isolde's premiere was scheduled for Vienna in 1859. However, the premiere was abandoned after some fifty-seven rehearsals, the musicians finding Wagner's score virtually impossible to learn and play, and the singers finding it unsingable. Its music was so revolutionary that Wagner was considered seriously insane, a musical anarchist and iconoclast intent on destroying Western music traditions. But the opera did have its premiere six years later and Wagner's ingenious harmonic innovations began to overtake the music world. After Wagner, many composers began to abandon tonality; it began a transformation in music's harmonic structure, such as the introduction of atonal, 12-tone, or serial music, an avant-garde technique that virtually considered conventional melody, rhythm and traditional harmony evil elements of the musical language.

Wagner's early operas, from *Die Feen* through *Lohengrin* (1850), reflect strong musical and aesthetic influences from the German Romantic as well as the Italian bel canto schools: those operas contain many parallels to the mysticism and spiritualism of Weber's *Oberon* (1826) and Marschner's *Der Vampyr* (1828), as well as the Italian bel canto masters, Rossini and Belllini.

Wagner vehemently opposed the abuses of the Italian bel canto school: their hackneyed librettos, obsession with spectacle, and showcases for singers: to Wagner, much of opera that preceded him was "causes without effects." Wagner shared Berlioz's description of the genre: "Music of the Italians is a sensual pleasure and nothing more. For this noble expression of the mind, they (the Italians) have hardly more respect than for the art of cooking. They want a score that, like a plate of macaroni, can be assimilated immediately without having to think about it, or even pay attention to it."

Nevertheless, Wagner's operas prior to 1850, particularly *Tannhäuser* and *Lohengrin,* possess intense lyricism and represent perhaps the pinnacle of the bel canto school: Wagner, at times the principal antagonist of Italian bel canto, ironically became its foremost and finest practitioner. But Wagner was seeking an antidote for the existing conventions of recitative, set-pieces, or numbers, that he considered elements that impeded the flow of the drama. In his next compositional period, beginning in the 1850s, he would develop theories of music drama that would completely transform opera traditions.

Wagner's challenge was to let drama run an unbroken course without restraining the action with purely musical forms. As such, he envisioned a complete fusion of drama and music, in which the drama would be conceived in terms of music, and the music would freely work according to its own inner laws, a balance in which the drama assisted but did not constrain the music. The words had to share equally with the music in realizing the drama, their inflections sounding ideally in alliterative clusters with the vocal line springing directly out of the natural rise and fall of the words. As such, the voices were to give the impression of heightened speech, and the ultimate opera would become a "sung drama."

However, where words failed, the orchestra would convey the drama through recurring musical themes, what Wagner called "motifs of memory," that were later termed leitmotifs.

In 1849, Wagner's participation in the Dresden political uprisings caused him to become exiled from Germany. He found safe haven in Zurich, where he began to pen his theories about opera: *Die Kunst und die Revolution* ("Art and Revolution"); *Die Kunst der Zukunft* ("The Artwork of the Future"); and *Oper und Drama* ("Opera and Drama"). Essentially, these were theories that envisioned the opera art form as a "Gesamtkuntswerk," a complete work of art that incorporated all artistic and creative elements: acting and gesture, poetry, music, and scenery; opera was idealistically a total artistic unity that was the sum of its various parts. As such, Wagner conceived opera as music drama: the full integration of text, music, and other artistic elements that contribute to realizing the drama.

Wagner's first attempt to put his theories and conceptions into practice began in 1848: he began his monumental trilogy, *Der Ring des Nibelungen* (The Ring of the Nibelung). In 1864, Wagner was rescued from financial disaster by Ludwig II, an impassioned admirer who had just acceded to the throne of Bavaria. With the King's support, Wagner produced *Tristan and Isolde* (1865), *Die Meistersinger* (1868), premiered the two *Ring* operas *Das Rheingold* (1869) and *Die Walküre* (1870), opened the Bayreuth Festspielhaus in 1876

Wagner's Ring and the Conquest of Will

Wagner's ancient mythological sources for his music-drama colossus, *Der Ring des Nibelung*, portrayed a turbulent world in which sinister and evil forces unconscionably lusted for power. He adapted the basic universal themes of those myths to create an allegory to deconstruct the moral values of his nineteenth-century century contemporary world: the *Ring*'s underlying conflicts and tensions expressed Wagner's moral outrage at the decadence and degeneration of his society's philosophical, political, social and economic values.

Wagner, like most contemporary nineteenth-century visionaries, considered himself a child of the previous century's Enlightenment, the heir to hopes and dreams that social progress and the ideals of human dignity would transform the evils and injustices of society. But the dream was shattered in the malaise following the French Revolution, when the restored authoritarian rulers of post-Napoleonic Europe became involved in a fiercely competitive struggle for political and economic power, heedless and reluctant to institute social reforms.

The Industrial Revolution had transformed society through its rapid changes in methods and mechanization; there was a new focus on machine rather than land. And in that transition new classes of society emerged. The bourgeoisie and middle classes became the new claimants to the old legitimacy, and a large class of working poor who were ignorant and illiterate, clamored for social progress. The old order of inherited title and property became involved in a battle for power against new forces that benefited from the industrial-capitalist system. A greater disparity arose between wealth and poverty, provoking deeper divisions to emerge in the social order. By the mid-nineteenth century, European society seemed to have become more profoundly divided by political, social, and economic realities; it was a division that created new claims to power, and ever more dramatically separated the dominators from the dominated, and the wealthy from the poor.

As Wagner viewed his contemporary society, he became a cultural pessimist, perceiving his world as decadent, immoral and unjust, a degeneration that was the result of an obsessive lust for material wealth and power that he considered the root of all evil. The *Ring* became Wagner's cri de coeur, his impassioned artistic expression of disdain and condemnation of society's vices and follies. In his saga, the protagonists — Gods, Giants and Dwarfs — are allegorically the decadent immoral forces of his contemporary society: the politicians, the authoritarian church, and the bourgeoisie, et al.

From inspiration to fulfillment, *The Ring* engaged Wagner for 26 years. During that long evolutionary period, his impassioned social critique became more profound and visionary as he became absorbed in the philosophical ideas of Ludwig Feuerbach and more specifically, Arthur Schopenhauer. In the *Ring*, the old order of Gods is destroyed in a cataclysm, what Wagner considered a necessary retribution for their despicable evil and the forced imposition of their Will. But Wagner concluded the *Ring* saga with a profound sense of hope, a sense of optimism in which the world had been redeemed and purified from its Curse of evil, and that a new sense of humanity would arise to inspire humanity toward a new moral order of lofty ideals and elevated conscience.

In Viking and Norse mythologies, magic rings were considered potent symbols of power, fortune and fame, as well as symbols of destiny; in their adverse form, if corrupted by greed, they were perceived as omens of tragedy and doom.

In all of Wagner's source sagas, three villainous forces are locked in eternal combat, all rivals to master and dominate the world: Gods, Giants, and Dwarfs. All of these forces are decadent and corrupt; in Wagner's *Ring*, they are symbolic representations of classes within the composer's 19th century contemporary society.

First, there is a race of Giants. They are symbols of the bloated bourgeoisie of Wagner's contemporary world, a class incapable of rising above the lowest form of materialism, but too indolent and too stupid to aspire to the ultimate prize of world-mastery; they desire only to live their lives in the protection and safety of their wealth.

Second, there are the Dwarfs, in particular, the evil Nibelung Dwarf Alberich, a force of unmitigated material lust who is obsessed with the acquisition of wealth and power. It is Alberich who steals the Gold in which riches and power are hidden, and by renouncing love, he is able to fashion the all-powerful Ring from the Gold, enslave the Nibelungs, and force them to amass his immense Hoard; with his newfound power Alberich intends to master the world and defeat the Gods and Giants. Alberich is the incarnation of all forces of materialism in society for whom money is synonymous with power; with his wealth, Alberich strives to become the wielder of infernal power.

Third, there are the Gods. They are the loftier spirits who bear the responsibility of rescuing the world from two threatening evils: Giants and Dwarfs. The Gods are allegorically the incarnation of corrupt nineteenth-century politicians or rulers of modern states. The Gods are ordained to use their power to maintain order and benefit the world. Wagner commented, to "bind the elements by wise laws and devote themselves to the careful nurture of the human race." But the Gods (any corrupt politician or ruler responsible for the injustices in the world) are morally flawed, unethical, and unscrupulous, achieving peace not by reconciliation and persuasion, but by force, cunning and deceit. Their supposed higher world order that is intended to evoke moral consciousness becomes absorbed by the evil against which they struggle; in the end, the Gods become as despicable and immoral as their enemies, a group who continually elevate self-interest above conscience and law.

The original Nibelungenlied deals primarily with the universal themes of lust, greed, and power. Although Wagner's ancient sources vary slightly in their specifics, certain aspects of the mythological accounts were common to all of them.

Alberich, a Dwarf, steals the Gold from the Rhine maidens, forges a Ring of power, and by upsetting the world's balance of power, incites the Gods and Giants to suppress him; after the Gods steal his Ring, he invokes a Curse on any possessor of the Ring. The Giants, Fafner and Fasolt, demand the Ring, Hoard, and Tarnhelm from the Gods in payment for building their Valhalla fortress; they carry off Freyja, the Goddess of love, as ransom. The youthful hero, Sigurd (Siegfried), slays Fafner, who had used the magic power of the Tarnhelm to transform himself into a Dragon; Sigurd acquires the Ring and the Hoard, but with it, its dooming Curse.

Sigurd falls in love with the Valkyrie, Brynhild, winning her from the fire that protected her enchanted sleep. But Grimhild, a sorceress and Queen of the Nibelungs, bewitches Sigurd into betraying Brynhild so that he can marry her daughter, Gudrun. Brynhild, now the possessor of the Ring gifted to her by Sigurd, seeks revenge and the return of her honor, but she is slain by the envious Nibelung Dwarf brothers who seek the all-powerful treasure.

In those myths, curses, magic, and sorcery represent powerful forces of doom and destiny. Heroes like Sigurd are blessed with magical weapons and arcane wisdom, and the Godhead, Odin (Wotan), is an arch-sorcerer who wanders the world disguised as a vagrant to gather information about world events (Wanderer). In some of the early sagas, the Valkyries were dark angels of death, or sinister spirits of slaughter, who soared over the battlefield like birds of prey to gather chosen heroes and bear them away to Valhalla, the heavenly fortress of Odin. In later Norse myth, the Valkyries were romanticized and became Odin's shield maidens, virgins with golden hair who served the chosen heroes mead and meat in the great hall of Valhalla. In the Volsung and Nibelungenlied sagas, the heroine Brynhild is idealized as a beautiful, fallen Valkyrie, more vulnerable than her fierce predecessors, and in many episodes, she falls in love with mortal heroes. And in the later myths, the tragedies of lovers rather than their heroic deeds are highlighted; as the hero Sigurd died, he called to his beloved Brynhild.

Thus, the Norse and German legends and myths provided Wagner with his underlying literary structure for his saga of *The Ring of the Nibelung.* Wagner would retain all of the myth's allegorical symbolism, but he would humanize their characters to make their story of lust, greed and power, a metaphor for his times.

Nevertheless, in many instances, Wagner was modifying his sources and creating a new myth. His most classic and ingenious innovations to his story were Alberich's renunciation of love that provided him with the secret to make the magic Ring from the Gold, and the introduction of Erda, the omniscient prophetess who awakens Wotan to his guilt. Wagner's original intent in *Siegfried's Death,* which ultimately became the final work, *Twilight of the Gods,* was that the sky god, Wotan, would receive Siegfried in Teutonic heaven (Valhalla), after the hero redeemed the world by transforming it into a classless society. However, Wagner could not betray his obsession with his archetypal heroines: Brünnhilde became that archetypal Wagnerian heroine, who redeems the world through her sacrificial suicide, and eliminates the Curse on the Ring by returning it to the Rhinemaidens; it is her noble sacrifice for the love of Siegfried that provides the prescription for the spiritual rebirth of the world.

In 1848, Wagner began to write a Prose Sketch entitled "The Nibelungen Myth as Scheme for a Drama," publishing it privately in 1853. By its final transformation it became a tetralogy that comprised the libretto and scenario for four music dramas: the title became *Der Ring des Nibelungen,* "The Ring of the Nibelung," or "The Nibelung's Ring." Ultimately, Wagner's four music dramas became *The Rhinegold* ("Das Rheingold"), *The Valkyrie* ("Die Walküre"), *Siegfried,* and *Twilight of the Gods* ("Götterdämmerung.")

Wagner wrote his four texts in reverse order, beginning with "Siegfried's Death," now *Twilight of the Gods,* and working backwards to explain earlier events: *Young Siegfried* became *Siegfried,* and eventually, *The Valkyrie,* and the *Prologue,* or *The Rhinegold.* Wagner himself called his epic a trilogy: a "Prologue" followed by three music dramas.

The music for *The Rhinegold* was begun in 1853, *The Valkyrie* in 1854, and *Siegfried* in 1857. But halfway through the second act of *Siegfried* Wagner laid down his pen for nine years, writing to Liszt: "I have led my Siegfried into the beautiful forest solitude. There I have left him under a linden tree and, with tears from the depths of my heart said farewell to him: he is better there than anywhere else."

Wagner had written himself to a standstill and needed stimulation from a totally different project: *Tristan und Isolde* and *Die Meistersinger* were composed during the interim. It is significant that when Wagner returned to *Siegfried*'s third act, his gear change is reflected with a blazing new creative energy: metaphorically, perhaps it represents Siegfried's — and to an extent Wagner's — rise to consciousness and awareness.

The *Ring*'s four music dramas are united by related musical material; some two hundred leitmotifs represent a massive vocabulary of musico-dramatic symbols and associations. By the time of the final episode, *Twilight of the Gods*, the listener can virtually follow the dramatic narrative by interpreting the meaning of its musical leitmotif symbols without the benefit of visual or verbal clarification. As such, Wagner's orchestra functions like a massive Greek chorus that narrates and comments on the action. In the *Ring,* Wagner proved his genius as both music dramatist and symphonist, composing elements in the music drama that have become indelible for the listener: *The Rhinegold*'s scene transitions and the "Rainbow Bridge" finale, *The Valkyrie*'s "Ride of the Valkyries" and "Fire music," *Twilight of the God*'s "Rhine Journey" and "Funeral music," and after Brünnhilde's "Immolation," the orchestral depiction of the downfall of the gods and the world's redemption.

Allegory denotes symbolic representation. The *Ring*'s leitmotifs are specifically symbolic representations, but they are presented in the language of music. It is through the emotive power of the musical language that ideas in the *Ring* are conveyed and responses are evoked; as such, the drama's characters, elements, and events become part of a complete mythography whose inner allegorical symbolism, in both words and music, provide intensely profound understanding as well as different levels of meaning. The symbolism of myth evokes intuitive rather than rational responses from the human psyche; Wagner's musical leitmotifs become those same symbolic images, often revealing and evoking profound inner thoughts and emotions. Ultimately, leitmotifs provided Wagner with the organic structure for his music drama, but more importantly, they provided the wherewithal to add profound impact to the drama through musical symbolism.

W agner was a man possessing profound intellectual curiosity; he was a voracious reader whose huge library of books, abandoned at the time of his 1848 exile, remains in Dresden. The *Ring* consumed Wagner over a vast creative period of 26 years, and inevitably, certain ideological conceptions of his massive undertaking were bound to change.

Initially, Wagner's sole intent in the *Ring* was to express his moral outrage at the evil values of his contemporary society: in metaphorical or allegorical form, he would parade all the decadent, degenerate, and philistine protagonists of his contemporary world, and ultimately destroy them in a cataclysmic apocalypse of fire and water. And, the victorious hero, Siegfried, would then succeed to Valhalla after recreating the world into a classless society. But over time, Wagner had evolved from the impassioned revolutionary of Dresden. Intuitively and rationally, he began to develop a different philosophical context for his saga that transcended the passions of his original cri de coeur and Sturm and Drang.

The German philosopher, Arthur Schopenhauer, had come under the spell of Orientalism when early in life he stumbled into a French translation of the Indian Upanishads; he became enthralled with Hindu and Buddhist doctrines regarding renunciation of the Will, or the extinguishing of desire. In "The World as Will and Idea"

(1818), Schopenhauer pitted Eastern mystical conceptions of wisdom against the Enlightenment's faith in reason, science, and civilization. Although his book remained unread for some 40 years, Europe's disillusionment after the 1848 Revolutions brought him a new and enthusiastic audience.

After Wagner became absorbed in the philosophy of Schopenhauer — the "renunciation of Will" — the essential conflicts of the *Ring* saga developed more profound meaning. Wagner had by now concluded that industrialized Europe would never escape or find release from its struggles: "I saw that the world was Nichtigkeit, a nothingness or an illusion." Thus, the *Ring*'s power conflicts were incontrovertible elements in the world's evolution, but he was now convinced more than ever that their cause was specifically humanity's blind exercise of Will.

Armed with Schopenhauer's preaching, Wagner found it necessary to revise his original conception for the conclusion of the *Ring*, and decided that it was necessary to destroy Wotan and the Gods in the final moments of *Twilight of the Gods*, instead of a victorious Siegfried ascending to Valhalla. Wagner commented about the fall of the Gods: "The necessity for the downfall of the Gods springs from our innermost feelings, as it does from the innermost feelings of Wotan. It is important to justify the necessity by feeling, for Wotan who has risen to the tragic height of willing his own downfall."

The Godhead Wotan had evolved into the indisputable tragic character of the *Ring* story, his agony the result of his insatiable Will as master the world. For Wagner, it was now necessary to conclude the *Ring* with the Schopenhauerian "renunciation of Will," a decisive condemnation of Wotan's Will — and all human Will — that he now believed was the cause of the world's evil. And similarly, Brünnhilde's sacrificial suicide and the purification of the Ring's Curse, would represent an acceptance of fate that finally released humanity from its endless cycle of desire, rebirth, and death. Thus, the *Ring*'s power conflicts were incontrovertible elements in the world's evolution, so the ultimate conclusion of the *Ring*, as well as the entire tragedy of *Tristan and Isolde*, became an expression of pure Schopenhauerian philosophy.

Schopenhauer directed his radical views about the renunciation of human Will to both Enlightenment and Christian ideology. In his conception, the Enlightenment had created a false optimism through its empty faith in reason and progress. He also condemned Christianity, which he concluded had urged men to strive for salvation in this world through a set of religious and moral preconceptions, which, he argued, posed the illusion of "Will as idea." Schopenhauer reasoned that the ultimate reality was that the exercise of human Will was purposeless, aimless, and neither reasonable nor rational: Will was simply a blindness that urged man to strive for meaningless goals such as their lust for wealth and power, and their achievement would ultimately cause anguish.

Schopenhauer proposed that man had to escape from the sickness and curse of the Will, a yearning that imprisoned him in a fatal state of eternal desire; they represented urges that man must extinguish, abandon, and renounce. Schopenhauer envisioned a new way of understanding the world that was immune from the remorseless desires of the ego, what he termed the destructive idea of the "world as Will." His resolution of the dilemma was for man to achieve salvation not through a religious or spiritual path, but through philosophic knowledge, compassion, and sympathy for others. And more importantly, that man could obtain a momentary release from life's curse of desire through aesthetic experience, such as viewing a painting or listening to a symphony; by experiencing the world in a new way — through moments of pure contemplation of art and music — man would become uncorrupted by contact with the gross materialism that surrounded him.

Schopenhauer's conception that music and art provided a way to transcend the Will's relentless grip — albeit temporarily — coincided with Wagner's belief that his music dramas would provide relief for restless souls. But Schopenhauer added intellectual profundity to Wagner's vision, and armed with his new philosophy, the composer became more convinced than ever that his music dramas would become a consecrated art form, and therefore, a transcendent musical experience.

In 1854, while Wagner was composing the music to the second act of *The Valkyrie*, he was deeply engrossed in Wotan's torment, an agony that was caused by the frustration of the Godhead's Will. Simultaneously, Wagner became immersed in the spell of Schopenhauer's philosophy, the idea that all human anxiety and conflict derived from self-imposed desires, or Will. Wagner began to realize what he had felt intuitively; that Wotan's inner conflicts derived from the frustration of his Will.

Wagner became mesmerized — and totally indoctrinated — by Schopenhauer's philosophy. He realized that the "renunciation of Will" had been a theme he had subconsciously brought to the surface in his earlier *The Flying Dutchman* and *Tannhäuser;* the idea that the world of active desire resulted in a suffering from which the soul yearned to be freed, and that freedom could only be achieved when the Will was extinguished. Later, Wagner's *Tristan und Isolde* (1863) became a testament to Schopenhauer's philosophy. (Wagner became so engrossed in Schopenhauerian philosophy, that he contemplated the opera, *Der Sieger*, a story centering on a disciple of Buddha.)

By applying Schopenhauer's philosophy of the "renunciation of Will," the essential conflicts of the *Ring* saga developed more profound meaning. Wagner had by now concluded that industrialized Europe would never escape or find release from its struggles: "I saw that the world was Nichtigkeit, a nothingness or an illusion." Thus, the *Ring*'s power conflicts were incontrovertible elements in the world's evolution, but he was now convinced more than ever that their cause was specifically humanity's blind exercise of Will.

B rünnhilde is the true heroine of the *Ring*, the synthesis of all of the Romantic era's ideals of love, wisdom, sacrifice, and redemption. Romanticists, and particularly Wagner, believed that man's most profound desire was to desperately seek human warmth and affection, and to give love and be understood through love: love was deemed the noble spirit that sustained the world and illuminated every human soul.

The keystone of all Wagner's operas is that man is ultimately redeemed through human love, an alternative path to salvation and redemption, that, like religious spirituality, raised consciousness to greater emotional and aesthetic sensibilities. But it was Goethe's ideal of the ennobled "holy woman" whom the Romanticists sought in their passionate pursuit of man's love-ideal: it was Goethe's glorification of the "eternal female" at the conclusion of *Faust*, "Das Ewig-weibliche zieht uns hinan" ("The eternal feminine draws us onward"), that became the rallying cry of German Romanticism; she was that intuitive, sacrificing woman whose love, understanding and wisdom provided the glorious path to man's redemption.

Goethe's eternal female became Wagner's "woman of the future," or "femme eterne," who, like Beethoven's Leonora in *Fidelio*, became the model for his idealized heroines: Senta (*The Flying Dutchman*), Elisabeth (*Tannhäuser*), Brünnhilde (*The Ring of the Nibelung*), and Isolde (*Tristan und Isolde*). These sacrificing women essentially provide unquestioning and unconditional love; as such, they redeem and heal man from his narcissism, ego, loneliness, isolation, desires, needs, and yearnings. Ultimately, the German Romanticists — and particularly Wagner — believed that man may strive through art or reason toward a synthesis of human experience, but it was woman's love alone that would lead him to achieving life's ultimate fulfillment. So for Wagner, woman's unqualified, sacrificing love became the ideal: in *The Flying Dutchman*, the condemned, egocentric, almost Byronesque Dutchman is redeemed through Senta's love, compassion, and ultimately her sacrifice; in *Tannhäuser*, the errant and tormented minstrel is redeemed not through his Pope, but through the love and sacrifice of Elisabeth.

The ultimate evil in the *Ring* is not necessarily Wotan's duplicity, but Alberich's renunciation of love, his negation of humanity's most profound aspiration; the entire drama concludes with the affirmation of the healing power of love. Therefore, Brünnhilde becomes the glorified heroine of the *Ring*, the idealized eternal female or "holy woman" whose insight, wisdom and love redeem the world by cleansing it from its Curse of evil.

Brünnhilde is that heroic female force that integrates all of man's yearnings. It is her love and wisdom that energizes Siegfried and raises him to consciousness, and she alone reconciles all the conflicts of the *Ring* through her sacrifice. In the finale of the *Ring*, the sacrificial consummation of her holy marriage is a magical moment that summarizes the entire essence of German Romanticism's eternal woman. Brünnhilde calls out to her magic steed, Grane: "Do you know where we go together? Does the fire's light on Siegfried draw you to it too? Siegfried, Siegfried, see how your holy wife greets you!"

Brünnhilde's immolation is a shattering moment, but a momentous affirmation of love as the world becomes purified from its Curse. Wagner seizes this moment as his music relentlessly modulates and interweaves significant leitmotifs, all triumphantly surging toward the towering prophecy of the world's transformation: Siegfried's heroic music fuses with the motive of the Fall of the Gods, and the motive of Redemption through Love provides the final transcendence. The Rhine banks flood, the flames ebb, and Hagen, whose monomania remains undaunted, plunges into the Rhine to seize the Ring, but is dragged to its depths by the Rhinemaidens. The Rhinemaidens reveal the Ring they have recaptured from Brünnhilde's ashes, now purified from its Curse. Above, Valhalla is ablaze, Wotan waiting for the transforming fires to destroy the Gods and end the old order.

The cataclysm does not signal the end of humanity, but rather, provides a glimmer of hope that suggests that a new generation will arise and be stirred to greatness through love and compassion: one cycle of humanity ended; another is ready to begin.

Wagner's *Ring* relates a profound story about crisis within the human soul, a portrait of that eternal conflict between nature and human nature.

Man is the maker of myths; *The Ring of the Nibelung* is Wagner's myth. In myths, human nature is ambivalent, a creature who is both great and flawed as he struggles between goodness and his destructive impulses. The *Ring* reaches deep into the abyss of the human soul, and in the end concludes that man indeed possesses the propensity for greatness, a grandeur he can achieve when his energies are transformed toward love and elevated moral conscience.

The evil Gods in the *Ring* acted to possess rather than protect, to conquer rather than to defend. The Gods were ordained to protect the world against evil, but when malevolent forces stole the secret of the Ring's power and threatened their power, the Gods became flawed, toppling the moral and ethical scales by becoming as deceitful and treacherous as the evil they were ordained to control. The peace that they presumed to have maintained was not achieved by persuasion and reconciliation, but by criminal acts involving force and guile; ultimately they sacrificed their morality for their own self-serving needs. Wagner cited their hypocrisy in his Prose Sketch, "The purpose of their higher world order is moral consciousness, but the wrong against which they fight attaches to themselves."

The human conflicts portrayed in the *Ring* are universal and timeless, a view into the human soul that possesses almost Biblical grandeur: avarice, greed, duplicity, fear, treachery and betrayal, incest, murder, hatred, and compassion and love. Wagner's *Ring* is a journey into the human soul. But the *Ring* portrays its conflicting landscape in the language of music, an evocative force that transcends the power of words and reaches into the very depths of the human soul, arousing and awakening emotions and sensibilities that are at times repressed in the dark human unconscious.

In the final moments of *Twilight of the Gods*, Wagner the poet was in conflict with Wagner the music dramatist; ultimately, he relied on his music to convey what the poet was trying to express in words. Originally, Wagner intended the omniscient Brünnhilde to utter a profound ode to love, but he decided to leave the gravity of those final moments to his musical language. Wagner's concluding music portrays a collision between all the conflicting forces of the *Ring*. Yet, his final musical statement is one of love, compassion and hope, a spiritual message proclaiming that universal faith in human love will elevate conscience, and promote those enduring ideals of wisdom, character, humility, courage, civility, and justice; the ultimate ideals necessary for humanity to survive.

Wagner commented on the entire essence of the *Ring*: "Every human being must be capable of feeling this unconsciously and of instinctively putting it into practice." ("Opera and Drama")

A Prologue to the *Prologue*

As *Das Rheingold* unfolds, its first 136 measures suggest the world's creation; it portrays a primordial wasteland of water in which surging arpeggios convey the water's flow and unceasing rise. Wagner was said to have remarked to Franz Liszt that his opening for *Das Rheingold* was like "the beginning of the world."

Wagner's Teutonic and Norse sources for *Der Ring des Nibelungen* contained a "genesis," a creation myth that explained the formation of the elements and the principal inhabitants of the world: Gods, Giants, and Dwarfs. With minor variations, those myths explain that in the beginning there was neither sea nor shore, nor heaven nor earth, but only Ginnungagap, a vast "yawning abyss" or "emptiness," which lay between the realms of fire and freezing cold. After fire melted the ice, warm air from the south collided with the chill from the north causing drops of moisture to fall into the gaping chasm of Ginnungagap. Over time, drops in the chasm caused more ice to melt, and the first life form evolved: Audhumla, the primeval cow.

From Audhumla's tears "flowed four rivers of milk" that nurtured Ymir, who was the first frost Giant, the implacable enemy of the Gods. Audhumla licked the salty ice that ultimately released Borr, or Buri. Borr married Bestla, the daughter of a frost Giant, and had three sons: Odin (Wotan), Vili, and Ve. The sons battled incessantly against the Giants. Finally, they slew Ymir, and then hurled his body into the center of the Ginnungagap.

Ymir's body gave birth to the world; his flesh became the earth, his bones formed the mountains, his teeth formed the rocks and stones, his hair formed the trees, his blood turned into the lakes and seas, and his skull formed the sky. Four Dwarfs, Nordi, Sudri, Austri and Westri, were formed from maggots in the rotting flesh of the slain giant, and then were condemned to life underground. Ymir's wounds flooded the land and drowned all his frost children, except his grandson, Bergelmir, who escaped with his wife and propagated the race of Giants.

The fierce Wotan made the human race from Ymir's body, which then inhabited the Midgard. But wars raged across the birthing world. Borr's sons, led by the godhead Wotan, struggled against the Giants. Wotan loved battle, and was the esteemed father of slain heroes, his name akin to fury or madness. He inspired men into battle by rousing them into a frenzied rage that caused them to fear nothing and feel no pain. Wotan and the gods raised a Hall of the Valiant — Valhalla, to which Valkyries would take the bravest human warriors after they were slain in battle. In Valhalla, the god presided over the resuscitated and resurrected heroes.

The Germanic gods feared their doom, a final struggle between the gods and the forces of evil that would resolve in a cosmic apocalypse; a "twilight of the gods," or Ragnarok. The catastrophe of the Ragnarok was inevitable and unpreventable, but did not signal the end of the cosmos: a new world was destined to rise again because two humans had taken shelter in Yggdrasil, the sacred tree of wisdom and knowledge; they emerged after the apocalypse and repopulated the earth.

Wotan's Spear represents the symbol of his moral power; on its shaft he engraved the Laws of human conduct. Wotan sacrificed an eye after he drank from the Well of Wisdom, symbolically turning inward and cultivating his soul with wisdom and knowledge; these were his first steps in the acquisition of consciousness and Will. Like Prometheus who daringly stole fire for mankind, and the Biblical story of Adam and Eve and the eating of the apple that brought knowledge, it was Wotan's drinking from the Well of Wisdom that represented his self-emancipation from nature and the end of innocence. In his new state of consciousness and separation from nature, he embarked on humanity's eternal struggle to control the forces of good and evil.

But in Wotan's new state of consciousness, he exercised his Will to control, rule, and even exploit the world. Wagner commented on Wotan's "sin" against nature and his rise to consciousness: "But error is the father of knowledge, and the history of the beginning of knowledge and error is the history of the human race, from the myths of earlier times down to the present day."

Principal Characters in Das Rheingold

Gods:

Wotan, the godhead	Bass
Fricka, wife of Wotan, goddess of marriage	Mezzo-soprano
Loge, god of fire	Tenor
Freia, goddess of eternal youth, sister of Fricka	Soprano
Donner, god of thunder, wind, lightning, brother of Fricka	Baritone
Froh, god of fields and rain, and brother of Fricka	Tenor
Erda, goddess of wisdom	Contralto

Nibelung Dwarfs:

Alberich, a smith	Baritone
Mime, brother of Alberich, a smith	Tenor

Giants:

Fasolt, brother of Fafner	Bass
Fafner, brother of Fasolt	Bass

Rhinemaidens:

Woglinde	Soprano
Wellgunde	Mezzo-soprano
Flosshilde	Mezzo-soprano

Das Rheingold Synopsis and Overview

The *Ring* cycle begins with *The Rhinegold*, designated a Prologue by Wagner: musical imagery portrays the world's creation; the cycle ends with the world's destruction. At the beginning there is a primordial wasteland in which there is water, and surging arpeggios convey its flow and unceasing rise. Wagner was said to have remarked to Franz Liszt that his opening for *Rhinegold* was like "the beginning of the world."

Water is a primal element from which, science claims, all life evolved. Instinctive early man was in harmony with nature; uncorrupted, unthinking, unaware, and wedded in a lost innocence and union with his natural world. But civilization progressed and evolved, and nature's creatures of instinct who were previously unencumbered by thought, broke their bonds and rose to consciousness; Prometheus daringly stole fire for mankind, and Adam ate the apple that brought knowledge. In his new state of consciousness, man became liberated and separated from nature, and proceeded to embark on humanity's eternal struggle between the forces of good and evil.

Wagner's *Ring* is populated by three human forces: Gods, Giants, and Dwarfs, all rivals locked in eternal combat in their pursuit of wealth and power; in their quest, they become corrupt, immoral, and degenerate.

These forces are metaphorically classes in 19th century industrialized Europe.

First, there is a race of Giants, symbolically the bourgeoisie, who are indolent, stupid, and aspire only to live in the protection and safety of their wealth.

Second, there are the Dwarfs, and in particular, the evil Alberich, who represents the incarnation of all forces of materialism. He possesses misdirected intelligence, and is evil and cunning, consumed only with the acquisition of wealth, power, and world domination.

Third, there are the Gods, headed by their supreme ruler, Wotan. He represents the incarnation of corrupt political power, and is supposedly modeled on the King of Saxony, Frederick Augustus I.

The Gods are lofty spirits who attempt to wield their power to maintain order and benefit the world; to "bind the elements by wise laws and devote themselves to the careful nurture of the human race." They are ordained to rescue the world from the threatening evils of the Giants and the Dwarfs, but in the process, they themselves become morally flawed, unethical, and unscrupulous, achieving their goals not by reconciliation and persuasion, but by using force, cunning, and deceit. The Gods strive for an exalted world order that is intended to invoke moral consciousness, but they elevate self-interest above conscience and become absorbed in the evil against which they fight; ultimately they become as despicably evil, villainous, and immoral as their enemies.

Scene 1: The Rhinemaidens, guardians of the Gold, praise the new-born world with innocence and sweetness: "wonder," "wander," "water."

The unsavory Alberich appears, the driving force in the *Ring:* he is the Nibelung Dwarf in the title, *The Ring of the Nibelung.* Alberich is ugly, awkward, and deformed, but behind his physical exterior he has human desires, and the Rhinemaidens cause sensations of love to rise within him. The maidens taunt and tempt him, and he pursues them with lust, but after they mock him with heartless contempt, their rejection of him transforms his desires into frustration, bitterness, and anger.

Alberich becomes distracted by the uncanny radiance of glowing Gold, and the Rhinemaidens tell him that a man who steals their Gold and fashions a Ring from it can achieve mastery of the world. Suddenly, the spurned Alberich's bitterness transforms into hope: if he cannot master the inner world of his yearnings and desires, with Gold and power he can master the external world; a wealth that can satisfy his desires by buying love from any mortal woman.

With indiscretion, the Rhinemaidens inform Alberich how to steal their Gold, coaxing him that if he renounces love, he can learn the secret that will enable him to fashion an all-powerful Ring from the Gold; with the Ring, he can achieve mastery over the world. Alberich, propelled by greed and power, accepts his destiny. In a terrifying moment, consciously and deliberately, he renounces love, and then steals the Gold; for Alberich, the Gold will become the ultimate resource he will use for evil purposes.

Wagner poured all the evils of capitalism into the creation of Alberich: the treasure he stole will become a means toward "measureless power"; the domination of society. Unable to find love, he deliberately rejected love altogether, and he will strive toward becoming a lawless totalitarian power, a destructive pursuit that will avenge his frustrations. With his new wealth, Alberich will vie for world power against Wotan and the Gods.

Scene 2: The God-head, Wotan, and his wife, Fricka, Goddess of wedlock, await their entry into their new impregnable fortress, Valhalla, built for them by the Giants, Fafner and Fasolt.

Wotan's Spear is the symbol of his moral power;. on its shaft are engraved the Laws of human conduct. He acquired his wisdom by drinking from the Well of Wisdom, his self-emancipation from nature, and his first step in the acquisition of consciousness. Immediately, he "sinned" by committing a willful and violent act against nature; he split a branch of the World Ash-Tree and engraved his Spear-shaft with Treaties amd Laws; thereafter, the Well dwindled and the despoiled and impoverished Ash-Tree died. Wagner commented on Wotan's "sin" against nature and his rise to consciousness: "But error is the father of knowledge, and the history of the beginning of knowledge on error is the history of the human race, from the myths of earlier times down to the present day." Nevertheless, Wotan ruled society with his Law-laden Spear that provided him "divine infallibility"; his conscious Will to control, sustain, rule, and even exploit the world.

In payment to the Giants for building Valhalla, Wotan promised Freia, the Goddess of eternal youth, a promise he disingenuously hoped he would not be called upon to honor. Wotan regards the Giants with contempt, coarse creatures of low intelligence, physically repulsive, but good laborers. When the Giants demand their fee, he is loathe to surrender Freia, for her golden apples provide the Gods with eternal youth.

Fricka, like Wotan, is a moral paradox, not free of ordinary human weaknesses, yet her God-role represents moral conscience. She reproaches Wotan for the levity with which he offered Freia to the Giants, as well as building the fortress to ensure his mastery of the world. However, Fricka indeed urged him to build Valhalla for purely selfish reasons, hoping that the new fortress would bind her errant husband more closely to home.

Loge, the crafty God of fire, amkes his long-anticipated arrival after having promised Wotan that then the time arose, he would contrive an alternative payment to the Giants.

Like all gods in mythology, Loge is ambivalent. As the fire God he is the patron of smiths, and the servant of man needing the benefits of fire. But in Norse mythology, Loge grew progressively evil, becoming a mischief-maker, an arch-trickster, and "The first father of falsehood." He was the son of Giants, and therefore a half-God or demi-God, who refers to himself in relation to the Gods, as "half as glorious as you glorious ones!", preferring to remain aloof from them, and an objective moral mirror of their consciences. Nevertheless, he despises the Gods, resents their superiority, satirizes them, relishes every opportunity to endanger them, exploits their needs and goals, manipulates them, and longs for their destruction.

Loge remains detached from the struggle between Gods, Giants, and Dwarfs, and seemingly has no ambition for power. Certainly, he has no respect for the Gods' solemn contracts, and is cynical when he addresses ethical issues. But symbolically, Loge represents pure intelligence, an attribute that enables him to see things clearly: therefore, of all the Gods, Wotan seems to be his only friend, and most in need of his artfulness. Loge appears in human form in *Rhinegold*; afterwards, he appears only as the elemental force of fire.

Loge arrives as the Gods' messenger of news. He relates that Alberich stole the Gold from the Rhinemaidens, that he has forged the Ring, and that he has enslaved the Nibelungs. His awesome story about the Ring's power tempts both the Gods and the Giants, but in particular, it arouses their fear that Alberich will turn that power against them. Loge suggests Alberich's Hoard as an alternative payment to the Giants; immediately, the Giants succumb to the lure and accept. As ransom, the Giants take Freia away, and as she disappears, the Gods suddenly find their youth and strength fading; they no longer have Freia's youth-preserving Apples. It only remains for Wotan, with the cunning help of Loge, to agree to steal the treasure form Alberich, pay the Giants, and rescue Freia.

Paradoxically, Fricka gladly and willingly approves of the forthcoming theft, inspired by a promise of golden trinkets for female adornment from the treasures of the Nibelungs. Wotan and Loge descend to Nibelheim to steal the Gold from Alberich.

Scene 3: In Nibelheim, Alberich has enslaved the Nibelung Dwarfs, and has forced his brother, Mime, to craft a Tarnhelm that will enable him to metamorphose into any shape, or become invisible. With wealth, might, and magical powers, Alberich is determined to dominate the world. But the magically endowed Tarnhelm becomes Alberich's undoing when Wotan and Loge coax him into making himself invisible, and capture him after he transforms himself into a toad. The victors, Wotan and Loge, ascend from Nibelheim with their victim, Alberich.

Scene 4: The defeated Alberich is forced to summon his Nibelung Dwarfs to surrender the Gold to the Gods. Wotan forcibly wrests the Ring from Alberich, but before departing, Alberich invokes a Curse of death upon anyone who shall possess the Ring, and envy to those who do not: it is a Curse that will haunt all future possessors of the Ring throughout the drama. Nevertheless, Wotan has become guilty of theft and deceit: he has stolen from a thief, but that does not condone his act of thievery.

The wise earth Goddess, Erda, appears, the prophetess whose wisdom provides her with foresight of the beginnings and ends of all things. She persuades Wotan to return the Ring, but also implies in riddles that the Gods will fall.

The two Giants, Fafner and Fasolt, quarrel over the Hoard, and immediately, Alberich's curse on the Ring is fulfilled: Fafner slays his brother and leaves with the Hoard, planning to disappear to a cave where he will protect the Hoard by transforming himself with the magic of the Tarnhelm into a Dragon.

The Gods enter their new fortress of Valhalla but Loge remains remote from them while he predicts their doom; in the Rhine below, the Rhinemaidens lament the loss of their Gold.

Wotan relishes his momentary glory but is fearful about the turn of events that threatens the power of the Gods and the world. He realizes that he must find a way to wrest the Gold from Fafner and return it to its primal innocence in the waters of the Rhine, thus cleansing the Ring of Alberich's curse. However, he cannot violate his Spear's Laws and act against Fafner using force, yet he must prevent Alberich from seizing the Ring, Tarnhelm, and Gold from Fafner.

Wotan contrives the idea of creating a hero, independent of his Will, who could overcome Fafner and rescue the treasure. His thoughts turn to a powerful Sword, a weapon possessing divine lineage and endowed with magical powers that will provide the needs for a future hero.

Story Narrative with Music Highlight Examples

Prelude:

The Prelude portrays a primordial wasteland at the beginning of creation that is dominated by water. Water is a primal element from which science claims all life evolved. In the musical introduction, the Rhine's waters gain strength and motion, and surging musical arpeggios suggest the water's flow and unceasing movement. As Wagner remarked to Franz Liszt, the musical imagery of the Prelude portrays "the beginning of the world."

The Waters of the Rhine

Scene 1: In the depths of the Rhine.

The misty lower depths of the Rhine are saturated with rock fissures and crags. Woglinde, a Rhinemaiden, greets the waters while swimming gracefully around a large rock whose peak is clearly visible in the upper waters. The Rhinemaidens praise the newborn world with childlike innocence and awe.

Greeting the Waters

Woglinde's sister Rhinemaidens, Wellgunde and Flosshilde, frolic merrily, but Flosshilde chides them for their carelessness in maintaining their vigil on the sleeping Gold which they protect.

While the Rhinemaidens delight in their innocent diversion, Alberich, a hunchbacked Nibelung Dwarf, emerges from a dark cavern and watches their frolicking with ever-increasing pleasure. He calls out to the Rhinemaidens, announcing that he comes from Nibelheim, the darkest caverns of the earth, which he would gladly abandon if he could share their merriment and love. The Rhinemaidens recoil and elude the unsavory visitor, mocking and rejecting him with heartless contempt, while reminding each other that their father warned them to beware of such ugly and repulsive creatures.

Alberich pursues the Rhinemaidens lustily. They taunt and tease him, causing sensations of love and desire to stir within him. When he tries to grasp one of the Rhinemaidens, he slips awkwardly on the slimy crags, prompting the maiden's laughter. Frustrated, his desires transform into bitterness. He loses his temper and condemns all of them, concluding that love will always elude him. Nevertheless, he continues to pursue them with a sensual fury, their defiance and evasion compounding his avenging passions: in his frustrated fury, he calls them "cold and bony fish" who should "take eels for their lovers."

Flosshilde pretends to take pity on the Dwarf and disarms him with cajolery and deception, promising him that he will be more successful with her than with her sisters; with her, he will enjoy the passions of genuine love. With feigned compliments, she tells Alberich, "Oh, the sting of your glance and your stiff scrubby beard, I would like to feel it forever! And might the locks of your hair, so shaggy and wild, float around Flosshilde forever! And your toad's shape and the croak of your voice! Oh, might I be dazzled and amazed to see and hear nothing else but these!"

Flosshilde heartlessly continues to taunt the Dwarf by first embracing him, and then brusquely rejecting him, prompting her sisters to burst into raucous laughter. Alberich becomes totally discouraged and enraged, vowing to seize at least one of them. As they elude him, he again slips awkwardly on the rocks. Derided and rejected, Alberich becomes furious, and then vengefully shakes his menacing fist at the Rhinemaidens.

Alberich's attention is suddenly drawn to a dazzling, radiant glow that he perceives in the waters above; it is the sleeping Rhinegold awakening.

The Sleeping Rhinegold

The Rhinemaidens gracefully swim around the Gold, praising its radiance with joy and rapture.

The Rhinegold

Rhein - gold! Rhein - gold! Leuchtende Lust,   wie lach'st du so hell und hehr!

Alberich, struck with awe, inquires about the Gold's significance. The Rhinemaidens invite him to join them to praise its magnificence, but he rejects their childish games. Nevertheless, he becomes aroused when they assure him that the Gold possesses limitless powers, and that anyone who wins the Gold and fashions a Ring from it would become master of the world.

The Ring

Flosshilde then admonishes her sisters to be discreet, reminding them that their father warned them to guard the Gold carefully lest a robber seize it, create a powerful Ring and use its powers for evil. But Wellgunde and Woglinde express their confidence that they have nothing to fear from this lascivious, lusting imp, a man who is visibly tormented and too preoccupied with his passion for love: they conclude that he would certainly never renounce love to obtain the secret to master a Ring from the Gold. Woglinde then reveals the secret of the Gold: "He who the power of love forswears, from all delights of love forbears."

Renunciation of Love

WOGLINDE

Nur wer der Min - ne Macht ent - sagt,   nur wer der Lie - be Lust ver - jagt,

Confidently, the Rhinemaidens assure themselves that no one in all creation would ever renounce the delights of love. Ironically, they invite Alberich to join them in their merriment, for the Gold's radiance even seems to have improved the imp's hideous form. Meanwhile, the spurned Alberich's bitterness transforms into hope as his eyes remain fixed solidly on the Gold, his devious mind contemplating the hidden secrets of wealth and power that he could obtain if he renounced love and fashioned the all-powerful Ring from the treasure: "Could I, through your magic, win the world's wealth for my own? If love is to be denied me, shall my cunning win me the Gold's delight? Keep mocking me! The Nibelung comes near your toy!"

Alberich cannot master the inner world of his yearnings and desires, but he can master the external world with Gold and power. Propelled by his lust for greed and power, Alberich reconciles himself to his newfound destiny. With a demonic laugh, he springs toward the summit of the rock and stretches out his hand towards the Gold. Solemnly and triumphantly, he rises to his destiny and renounces love: "My hand quenches your light. I wrest the Gold from the rock, and will fashion the Ring of revenge. Hear me flooded waters: henceforth love shall be accursed forever!"

The Rhinemaidens scatter in terror. Alberich seizes the Gold and plunges with it into the depths of the Rhine. As he disappears from sight, his sinister mocking laughter is heard against the lamenting cries of the Rhinemaidens.

Scene 2: On a mountain height

As day dawns, the waves of the Rhine gradually transform into clouds. A fine mist slowly disperses to reveal a bright, open area atop a mountain. Visible in the background is the majestic, newly built fortress of Valhalla. In the foreground Wotan, the godhead, and Fricka, his wife and goddess of marriage, sleep on a flowery bank; the broad Rhine flows between them and the fortress.

Wotan dreams blissfully of the splendid fortress that has been built for the gods: a majestic, impregnable stronghold and testament to his power from where he will rule the world with might and eternal glory. He conceived the citadel in his dreams and caused its completion through his undaunted Will.

Valhalla

Fricka, like Wotan, is a moral paradox. As a goddess she represents moral conscience, but she is not free of ordinary human weaknesses. She does not share her husband's illusions about power, for what fills him with pride, overcomes her with fear and dread. She rouses Wotan from what she calls his "deceptive dream," exhorting him to become realistic about the crisis she senses will soon overcome the gods.

Fricka is perturbed because Wotan failed to consult with her and the other gods before making what she considered a ludicrous contract with the Giants to build Valhalla. Wotan callously and capriciously promised to pay the Giants with Freia, her sister and goddess of love, whose golden apples sustain the gods' eternal youth. Fricka chides Wotan for his heartlessness and levity in sacrificing the goddess of love and youth for "the garish toy of empire and power."

Wotan assuages his wife's anxiety, assuring her that in truth he never intended — nor does he intend — to surrender Freia to the Giants; after all, Freia's golden apples provide eternal youth to the gods.

Wotan's Laws, Treaties, and Compacts

Wotan calms Fricka's fears, admonishing her that he has entrusted Loge, the cunning and unscrupulous god of fire, to fulfill his promise to find an alternative payment to the Giants when the hour of reckoning arises. He regards the Giants with contempt, considering them coarse and physically repulsive creatures of low intelligence, but good laborers. He further reproaches Fricka's hypocrisy, reminding her that she indeed favored the building of Valhalla: Weren't Fricka's motivations self-serving? Didn't she believe that the new fortress would keep her errant and philandering husband at home?

Marital Fidelity

FRICKA

Herrliche Wohnung, wonniger Hausrath, sollten dich binden zu säumender Rast.

As they speak, Wotan's sister-in-law Freia arrives, breathless and frightened.

Freia

Terrified, Freia pleads with Wotan and Fricka for help. Now that Valhalla is finished, the Giants want their pay, and Freia is defenseless against the Giants who are pursuing her. Wotan calms her fears with assurances that Loge will soon arrive to resolve the problem of payment to the Giants.

Fricka scornfully reproaches Wotan for his continued trust in that despicable trickster who has continually caused harm to the gods. Wotan defends Loge, self-assured in his confidence that when wisdom fails, the intelligent Loge's artfulness and cunning will succeed. Wotan continues to have unbounded faith in the wily rogue. After all, although Loge initially advised him to pledge Freia to the Giants in payment for Valhalla, he also assured Wotan that he would find the means to annul the promise.

Freia, convinced that Wotan is sacrificing her to the Giants, calls desperately for help from her brothers, Donner and Froh. Fricka compounds Freia's distress by telling her somberly that the godhead has woven a net of treachery about her and has forsaken her.

The Giants, Fasolt and Fafner, arrive, treading noisily while brandishing large clubs.

Giants

Fasolt seems gentler in nature than his fiercer brother, Fafner, and genuinely has tender feelings for Freia. Fafner, who is more uncouth and brutish than his brother, envisions Freia for what she represents: the assurance of eternal youth. Fasolt respectfully and patiently requests Freia as their promised payment, explaining that the Giants toiled endlessly, and untiringly piled heavy stones upon heavy stones in order to build Valhalla.

Wotan contemptuously refuses their demand for Freia. He denounces their request as ludicrous and asks them to suggest another payment. Fasolt becomes confounded, and inquires if the solemn Laws engraved on Wotan's Spear are nothing more than a mockery. But Fafner, more realistic, sneeringly advises his brother that the godhead's failure to honor their contract is another example of his unscrupulousness.

Solemnly, Fasolt warns Wotan of the consequences if he fails to honor their agreement, reminding the god that his power rests in his virtue in honoring his treaties; if he renounces his promise, his wisdom shall be cursed, and the peace between the Giants and the gods will end forever. Wotan waves Fasolt's admonition airily aside, informing him that the contract for Freia was made in jest; certainly boors like the Giants are unable to appreciate the beautiful goddess's charm and grace.

Angrily, Fasolt accuses Wotan of mocking the Giants. He repeats their agreement, explaining that they toiled hard solely because they wanted the reward of a beautiful woman and her assurance of eternal youth. As Fasolt speaks of Freia's charm and grace, his coarseness transforms into tenderness. But the more brutal Fafner interjects contemptuously, admonishing his brother to cease arguing with the arrogant and unscrupulous god: they will take Freia, and the gods will be doomed, because without Freia's youth-perpetuating golden Apples the gods will age, weaken, wither and die.

Freia's Golden Apples

Gold' - ne Äp - fel   wachsen   in   ih - rem Gar - ten,

Wotan becomes restless, fearful and anxious, wondering why Loge has not arrived yet to resolve his dilemma. Meanwhile, he again asks the Giants to demand another wage, but Fasolt again refuses. As both Giants try to seize Freia, she runs to her brothers, Donner and Froh. Froh, the god of fields and rain, places a protecting arm around Freia, and Donner, the god of thunder, stands before the Giants, brandishing his hammer threateningly. Freia continues to complain that the gods have forsaken her. Wotan intervenes and commands all to cease their quarreling. He places his Spear between the disputants and implores the Giants to trust him by assuring them that he is bound by the rules of his Law-laden Spear; if he were to break a single Treaty, his power would be ended forever.

Wotan's Spear

Angry, disgusted and frustrated, Wotan looks anxiously toward the valley for the arrival of Loge. Suddenly, he sees a sparkle of flame, and then a nimble figure that approaches, leaping from one rock to another.

Loge, the crafty demi-god

Wotan sighs in relief as Loge finally arrives.

Loge is the son of Giants, and therefore, a half-god, or demi-god; he refers to himself in relation to the gods as "half as glorious as you glorious ones!"

As the god of fire, Loge is the patron of smiths, and the servant of man needing the benefits of fire. Loge is cunning, artful, and full of malicious mischief, a restless, elusive spirit, who sweeps homeless through the world, wandering wherever his whims lead him.

Loge remains seemingly detached from the struggle between Gods, Giants, and Dwarfs, and expresses no outward ambition for power. He prefers to remain aloof from the gods so that he can be an objective moral mirror of their consciences.

Loge represents pure intelligence, an attribute that enables him to see issues with clarity. As such, of all the gods, Wotan seems to be his only friend, and most in need of his talents.

Wotan confronts Loge to fulfill his promise to find a substitute payment to the Giants instead of Freia. Loge glibly raises his hands in cynical protest, denying that he made any such promises. Wotan reproves Loge's elusiveness, roguishness, and trickery, cautioning him that he should beware not to deceive him. The duplicitous Loge protests that all he had promised was that he would ponder the problem and consider a solution. Nevertheless, he has truly devoted his serious energy to resolving their problem, searching unceasingly through the world for a substitute ransom for Freia that might satisfy the Giants.

Wotan reacts to Loge's explanation with skepticism. Fricka angrily reproaches Wotan for placing faith in this treacherous knave; Froh tells him that he should be called "not Loge but Lüge" ("lies"); and Donner threateningly vows to destroy his power. Wotan steps between the feuding gods and Loge to make peace, and diplomatically admonishes them not to affront his friend; after all, he assures them, the slower he is to give counsel, the craftier his insight and advice. Loge, however, remains contemptuous, claiming that their accusations against him are merely subterfuges for their own gross duplicity.

Loge then proceeds to relate the events surrounding Alberich's theft of the Rhinegold. The sorrowful Rhinemaidens told him how the Nibelung Dwarf, having sought their favors in vain, solemnly renounced love so he could fashion the all-powerful Ring, and then robbed them of the Gold; with Alberich's newfound power, he has enslaved the Nibelung Dwarfs and forced them to mine his Hoard from the Gold. The Rhinemaidens implored Loge to seek Wotan's help in punishing the thief, recover their Gold, and return it to the waters from where it had been ravished. Loge proudly compliments his integrity, he has kept his promise to the Rhinemaidens and has related their loss and grief to the gods.

But Wotan is indifferent to Loge's story, and at this time, he is more concerned with his own pressing needs to find an alternative to pay the Giants than with the Rhinemaiden's dilemma of their ravished Gold. However, Loge's revelation about the stolen Gold does provoke and unsettle the Giants: Fasolt condemns the Nibelung Dwarf as their enemy, and one who has always evaded their grasp; Fafner expresses his conviction that with the Dwarf's newfound powers, he will be brewing mischief for all of them.

Capriciously, Fricka asks if the Gold provides adornment for women. Loge, with his usual craftiness, explains that the woman who possesses the Nibelung's golden trinkets could ensure her husband's faithfulness. Loge's revelation prompts Fricka's enthusiasm. Motivated by the fact that the Gold might provide a possible solution to her marital problems, she turns to Wotan and urges him to win the treasure.

Loge further explains that because Alberich has fashioned the all-powerful Ring, he is impregnable and beyond their reach. Loge's revelation causes fear and terror to overcome the gods: Donner predicts that they will all become enslaved by the Dwarf Alberich if the Ring is not wrested from him; Wotan fully recognizes the ominous power Alberich now possesses; and Froh expresses his confidence that the gods can seize the Ring from Alberich.

Loge concurs with Froh and proposes his plan: "By theft! What a thief stole, you can steal from the thief. Could anything be clearer? But Alberich guards himself with cunning weapons; to return the lustrous Gold to the Rhinemaidens, you must be shrewd and wary in order to surpass his wiles." Wotan echoes Loge with an expression of disbelief: "Return it to the Maidens?" Fricka, the goddess of marriage, supports the gods contemplation of theft, renouncing the ugly brood of Dwarfs who have used their wiles to lure so many women unwillingly to their lair.

Suddenly, all the gods become silent. Each ponders their reasons and willingness to become an accomplice in forcibly wresting the Gold and Ring from Alberich, except for Wotan, who is unconvinced and expresses his reservations, fearful of achieving their goals through wrongdoing.

The Giants intervene in the gods' dilemma: Fafner announces that the Gold would be a better alternative as payment to the Giants than Freia. Although Fasolt is initially unwilling to surrender his dreams of possessing the gracious and beautiful Freia, both Giants trudge before Wotan and announce their decision; they will relinquish their claim to Freia if they are paid with the Nibelung's Gold.

Wotan indignantly protests that their request is ludicrous. How could he pay them with Gold that he does not own? And further, do they expect him to conquer Alberich, seize the Gold, and then casually deliver the treasure to the Giants? Wotan despairs, realizing that satisfying the Giants by conquering the Nibelung represents a distasteful and unjust solution to his dilemma.

But the god is caught in a trap, the result of his own carelessness, disingenuousness, and duplicity. In truth, Wotan never intended to surrender Freia because he trusted Loge's craftiness to find him an alternative payment. His sole purpose in making the contract with the Giants had been to fulfill his lofty dream to build Valhalla, a fortress from which he would maintain order in the world by bending both the Giants and Nibelungs to his Will. But now Wotan fears that the Dwarf Alberich threatens him — and peace in the world — and will use the Ring to master the universe. Wotan becomes convinced that Alberich must be defeated, and that the gods are justified in using force and deceit: he must fight fire with fire and evil with evil; a sacrifice of conscience and justice that he must make for the greater good of the world.

Suddenly, Fasolt brusquely draws Freia to his side and orders her to remain with them until the ransom of Alberich's Gold is paid. Freia will remain their hostage until nightfall, and if the Nibelung's Gold is not tendered to them by that time, the gods will forfeit her forever. Freia is thrown across their shoulders and screams in vain as she is forcefully dragged away.

As Freia disappears, the gods suddenly transform, becoming old and pale, seemingly sick, wrinkled and withered. Froh's boldness and courage desert him; Donner's arms become feeble and he is unable to hold his great hammer; and Fricka has now grown old and gray.

Cynically and unsparingly, Loge observes the transformation of the gods and describes the terrifying reality that has overcome them: without Freia's golden Apples, the gods' youth and strength have faded, the tree branches have drooped, and decaying fruit has fallen to the ground. Loge is immune to their misery because he is only a half-god, one who does not need their delicate youth-preserving fruit. Loge gloats as he witnesses the gods' dilemma and forecasts their impending doom.

Fricka reproaches Wotan as the cause of the gods' horrible predicament, their present shame and disgrace. She rouses Wotan and prompts him to act with resolve. Wotan raises his Spear and announces his decision that the gods will secure Freia's ransom. He bids Loge to join him to assault Nibelheim and seize Alberich's Gold. Cynically, Loge cruelly taunts Wotan, reminding him that his lofty purpose should be to rescue the Gold and return it to the Rhinemaidens, but Wotan contradicts him furiously, explaining that his sole purpose is to secure Freia's ransom. Loge continues to taunt Wotan with his sarcasm, suggesting that they descend to Nibelheim through the Rhine, but Wotan refuses, preferring to avoid meeting the lamenting Rhinemaidens.

As a sulphurous vapor rises, Wotan and Loge disappear into a fissure in the rocks and proceed to descend into the caverns of Nibelheim.

Scene 3: Nibelheim

In Nibelheim, the thunderous, frenzied, rhythmic sounds of hammering on anvils musically portray the enslaved Nibelung Dwarfs forging Gold for Alberich.

Hammering of the Nibelungs

The vapor recedes and reveals a dark, rocky, subterranean chasm. A red glow from the smith's fires illuminates Wotan and Loge as they enter Nibelheim.

Since Alberich seized the Rhinegold and fashioned the Ring, he has enslaved all the Nibelung Dwarfs, brutally forcing them to mine more gold and more treasure from the bowels of the earth.

Lament of the enslaved Nibelungs

The din of the hammering smiths rises to a loud crescendo and then gradually dies away. Alberich appears while dragging his shrieking brother Mime. To overcome his fears of being robbed of the Ring, Alberich commanded Mime, the most skilful of the Nibelung smiths, to mold a Tarnhelm, a magic helmet that can make anyone who wears it metamorphose into any shape or become invisible. Mime swears that he has been unsuccessful in molding the Tarnhelm. However, Alberich suspects that his brother has indeed fashioned the magic helmet, but is concealing it from him in the hope that he will use it himself to overcome his stronger brother. Alberich threatens Mime to produce the helmet by brutally beating and thrashing him. Mime makes stumbling excuses, admitting that the work is indeed finished but that he has been holding it back to see if it warrants improvement. In his fright he lets the delicate magic helmet fall. Alberich immediately seizes it, takes it in his hand, examines it critically, and delights in his discovery of the long-sought Tarnhelm.

Tarnhelm

Alberich places the Tarnhelm on his head and tests its powers by invoking a spell: "Night and darkness - nowhere seen!" At once, to Mime's astonishment, Alberich disappears, leaving only a cloud of vapor appearing where he was standing. When Mime inquires about the whereabouts of his brother, the invisible Alberich proceeds to thrash him unmercifully.

Still only visible as a column of vapor, and even more confident of his powers, Alberich imperiously announces to the Nibelungs that they are his slaves forever, and viciously commands them to kneel before their master. He further admonishes them that they must dutifully tend to their work, because with his new magical powers he will be scrutinizing them in invisible form. Alberich roars, curses, whips the Nibelungs, and then disappears. The slaves begin their frenzied hammering amidst howls and shrieks. Mime groans, wails, and sinks to the ground in pain and terror.

When Wotan and Loge arrive, they discover the whimpering Mime and raise him to his feet. In answer to their inquiries, the Dwarf relates the history of the Nibelung's sad fate; that his brother Alberich forged a Ring from the ravished Rhinegold, and that with its power he has enslaved the entire Nibelung race, vanquishing their once innocent happiness in which they forged trinkets and toys for their womenfolk. Now, the brutal Alberich uses the Ring's magic power to locate the Gold, and then forces the Nibelungs to mine, melt, cast it into bars, and heap it into mounds. Mime reveals that he succeeded in making the Tarnhelm, but that he was unaware of the secret spell that could animate it. Mime despairs: a fool who has been punished for his labors.

Mime's Despair

Wotan and Loge laugh at the grotesque and lamenting Mime. The Dwarf is bewildered and inquires as to their identity. Wotan and Loge assure him that they are friends who have come to liberate the Nibelungs. Suddenly, Alberich is heard approaching. Mime runs about wildly in helpless terror and urges the strangers to be on their guard.

Wotan seats himself while Loge remains by his side. Alberich enters briskly from the inner caverns, now transformed back to his own shape, and with the Tarnhelm hanging from his side. He whips a throng of frightened Nibelungs who are laden with metalwork that they pile up in a huge mound. Then, he orders them to return to the mines and dig for more gold. He draws the Ring from his finger, mutters a mysterious incantation, and immediately the shrieking Dwarfs, including Mime, scatter and flee from him in terror.

Servitude

Alberich halts suspiciously before the two strangers. He brandishes the Ring threateningly, admonishing them to tremble in terror before the great lord of the Ring.

Warily and distrustfully, Alberich scans the intruders and inquires the reason for their presence in Nibelheim. Wotan replies that they have heard about his great achievements and power and have come to witness them. With cajolery, Loge reminds Alberich of their earlier friendship; after all, he is none other than the fire-god who has brought comforting warmth to the Dwarf's sunless cave, and brought fire for his forges. Alberich refuses to be duped, recalling that the duplicitous Loge once pretended to be his friend, but now consorts with the "light-elves" who dwell above. (*Lichtalben,* the light-elves; Alberich himself is a *Schwarzalb,* a black-elf.) Alberich reveals that he no longer fears Loge because his power now rests in his Hoard; what they see is trivial, for day by day his Hoard grows and increases his glory and power.

Wotan inquires what value his wealth provides in the caves of Nibelheim where the Hoard can buy him nothing. Alberich boasts that his treasure provides the power to bend the whole world to his will; he will transform the gods into his vassals, and those who live, laugh and love on earth, will be deprived of happiness. He boasts that he has renounced love, and at his command all humanity shall renounce love because they will yearn for wealth and power: Alberich's Ring and the great Hoard he has amassed through its powers. And those despicable, deceitful gods who dwell in bliss in majestic Valhalla must beware, for their power will crumble before the might of the Nibelung's Ring and Hoard; and all women who once despised the ugly Dwarf will yearn to satisfy him.

The Hoard

Alberich has revealed his inner soul: he is the incarnation of hatred and evil Will, a destructive yet powerful force that gods and men will have to reckon with. Alberich's contemptuous laughter provokes Wotan's outrage, but Loge intervenes to restrain the godhead, and advises him to control his anger. Loge proceeds to placate Alberich with his usual smooth assurances. He compliments Alberich's wonderful achievements that have provided him with limitless power, and have forced all the Nibelungs to kneel before him.

With deferential care, Loge hints that Alberich should be cautious not to let his envious Nibelungs revolt and destroy him. He suggests that while the Ring remains in Alberich's possession his power is secure, but he would be vanquished if a thief stole the Ring from him while he slept. Loge cunningly appeals to Alberich's vanity, and the evil Dwarf falls into his trap. Alberich replies arrogantly that he has cleverly foreseen danger and has protected himself with the Tarnhelm, a magic helmet which can change his shape or make him invisible at will.

Urged on by the cunning Loge, Alberich's magically endowed Tarnhelm will become his undoing. With pretended awe, Loge compliments Alberich's Tarnhelm as perhaps the greatest marvel of the universe, an additional implement to insure his eternal might and power. Loge coaxes Alberich's egotism by goading him to demonstrate his ingenious wonder. The vain Dwarf becomes willing and eager to prove his wizardry, and asks Loge what shape he would like him to assume. Loge makes no choice, casually telling him that the deed confirms the word. Alberich obliges, places the Tarnhelm on his head, and murmurs a spell: "Dragon dread, turn and wind." Instantly, Alberich disappears; in his place, a huge serpent writhes on the ground, stretching its gaping jaws towards Wotan and Loge.

The Serpent

Loge pretends to be paralyzed with terror and pleads for mercy; Wotan breaks into hearty laughter and ironically compliments Alberich on his wondrous magic. The serpent vanishes and Alberich reappears in his own form, eagerly seeking their praise for his spectacular feat. Loge assures him that he has proven himself, and that they can no longer be skeptics about his magic powers. Loge again feigns admiration for Alberich and then cunningly invites him to perform a smaller transformation, advising the Dwarf that in a smaller size he could more easily escape potential danger.

Vainly, Alberich agrees to accommodate Loge's request, but inquires how small he wants him to become. Loge replies that he should become small enough to creep into a toad's crevice. Alberich, reveling in the simplicity of the request, murmurs his spell once again, and in his place a toad appears. At a quick word from Loge, Wotan immobilizes the toad with his foot, and Loge takes it by the head and seizes the Tarnhelm. Instantly, Alberich becomes visible, transformed back to his own shape and form.

Alberich curses them while struggling helplessly. Loge binds him with a rope. They drag the bound Alberich to the shaft from which they entered Nibelheim, and the three of them disappear.

Scene 4: The mountain heights

Wotan and Loge ascend from Nibelheim with their captured victim. Alberich furiously belittles himself for his foolishness and blind trust, and admits that he has learned his lesson; he will be wiser and less disingenuous in the future. Loge goads him sarcastically, gleefully dancing about the captive Dwarf and provoking Alberich to curse and vow revenge against the rogue and robber. Alberich demands his freedom, which Loge promises him after Alberich surrenders all the Nibelung's treasure.

Alberich, in an aside, comforts himself by reasoning that if he can save the Ring he can recreate the Hoard. He announces that he will summon the Hoard for them if they will untie his hand. As Loge frees his right hand, the Dwarf places the Ring to his lips and murmurs a secret command that summons the Nibelungs, who emerge from the clefts and begin to amass the Hoard. Alberich, ashamed and disgraced by his bondage, hides his face as he imperiously orders his enslaved Nibelungs to be quick with their work and not look upon him. He again kisses his Ring and holds it out commandingly, causing the terrorized Nibelungs to flee back into the clefts.

After the Hoard is amassed, Alberich demands his release and asks for the Tarnhelm to be returned to him, but Loge bluntly advises him that it must remain with them. Alberich curses him, but consoles himself with the knowledge that he can again force Mime to make another Tarnhelm.

Wotan then demands Alberich's Ring. Alberich cries out in desperation, offering his life but not the Ring. Wotan becomes insistent and asks Alberich how he came to possess the Ring, and where he found the Gold to fashion the Ring, all the while knowing the truth about his theft. Alberich suddenly has a revelation and realizes that his captors are the duplicitous gods; intuitively he realizes that their intentions are to steal his Ring that will secure their power. He weighs the moral scales between himself and the gods and reasons that both share a common purpose; he concludes that the gods themselves would have stolen the Gold from the Rhine had they known how to forge the Ring from it.

On the scale of morality Wotan and Alberich are in perfect balance. Nevertheless, Wotan cannot withdraw because he is irrevocably committed to his course of wrongdoing, caught in a net of his own weaving in which he is yet unable to foresee the horrifying consequences of his actions.

Wotan wants the all-powerful Ring, and ruthlessly flings himself on the Dwarf and tears it from his finger. The god, like Alberich, has become possessed with the power inherent in the Ring. He places the Ring on his finger, contemplates it, and revels that it now belongs to him; with the all-powerful Ring, he now is the incontestable ruler of the world.

Alberich, with a horrible shriek, laments his ruin, prompting Wotan to give Loge permission to release the impotent Dwarf. Loge dutifully unties Alberich and informs him he is free to leave. Alberich greets his freedom with a wild and contemptuous laugh, and then condemns his assailants by invoking a horrifying Curse on the Ring.

Curse on the Ring

Wie durch Fluch er mir ge-rieth,   verflucht sei die - ser Ring!

Alberich's Curse condemns any possessor of the Ring; that each possessor of the Ring shall become consumed with torment, misfortune, harm, anxiety and death. And those who do not possess the Ring, shall be destroyed by envy.

Torment and Misfortune

With a demoniacal laugh, Alberich disappears into the clefts. Cynically, Loge asks Wotan if he heard the Dwarf's fond farewell. Wotan disregards Alberich's Curse, his thoughts totally consumed by the power inherent in the Ring that he now possesses.

The Giants return with Freia, followed by Fricka, Froh and Donner. Fricka rushes to Wotan and anxiously asks him for news about his mission into Nibelheim. Wotan points to the Hoard and assures her that by force and guile the gods were victorious, and that Freia's ransom has been secured. With Freia's return, the gods' youthful freshness is restored.

Wotan offers the Giants the Nibelung Hoard as payment for Freia's freedom. At first, Fasolt becomes reluctant, saddened at the thought of relinquishing Freia, but then decides that if he must lose her he wants the treasure heaped so high that it will hide her from his sight. The two Giants thrust their staves in the ground on either side of Freia to measure the Hoard they want amassed for them. Wotan, sick with a sense of shame and degradation, bids that they proceed quickly. The Giants heap up the Hoard between two staves, assisted by Loge and Froh, while Fafner, in his frenzied greed, searches for crevices, and packs the pile more tightly so that more Gold can be amassed.

Wotan turns away in profound disgust, commenting that he feels disgraced. Fricka adds to his torment by reproaching him for his ambitious folly of building Valhalla. As Fafner cries out for more Gold, Donner circles about him furiously, threatening the greedy Giant with his hammer. Loge assures the Giants that they have the entire Hoard, but when Fafner peers more closely at the dense pile he is able to see Freia's golden hair through an opening. He immediately demands that the Tarnhelm be thrown in to fill the void. Wotan, ever more disgusted, reluctantly orders Loge to add the Tarnhelm to the pile to fill the crevice.

Fasolt, still grieving that Freia will no longer be his prize, peers more closely at the heap and laments that there still exists a gap through which he can see Freia's shining eyes. Loge protests that it cannot be filled because the Hoard is quite exhausted, but Fafner points to the Ring on Wotan's finger and demands that it be used to plug the gap. Loge assures Fafner that Wotan intends to return the Ring to the Rhinemaidens from whom the Gold was ravished, but Wotan contradicts him, swearing adamantly that he will not yield the Ring to anyone. Loge protests that Wotan has reneged on his original promise to return the Ring to the Rhinemaidens. Wotan defends his decision to keep the Ring, denying that he is bound by any promises made to Loge, and then turns to Fafner and urges him to make a substitute request.

Fasolt angrily pulls Freia from behind the pile. He accuses the gods of reneging on their promise, and as such, they have forfeited Freia forever. Fasolt begins to leave, but Fafner holds him back. Fricka, Donner, and Froh appeal to Wotan to relent, but he has become intransigent, too overcome by the idea of possessing the Ring and its power. He again proclaims that he will not yield the Ring, and turns away from them in blind, furious anger, remaining impervious both to the Giants who threaten to abduct Freia, and the pleas of the other gods.

The present crisis of the gods can only be resolved by the intervention of a world force greater than even the godhead Wotan himself. Darkness suddenly descends and a bluish light appears from a rocky cleft: Erda, the goddess of earth and wisdom, becomes visible as she rises from below the ground to half her height. Erda is the mother of the Norns who weave threads that prophesy the world's destiny. She is a prophetess whose wisdom provides her with the knowledge of the past and the future of the universe. Erda cautions Wotan and advises him to return the Ring to the Rhinemaidens:

Erda, goddess of wisdom

The gods stand in awe and become speechless. Erda stretches out her hand commandingly to Wotan, again bidding that he relinquish the Ring to evade the Curse pronounced on it. Erda, the woman who possesses the entire world's wisdom, confounds Wotan by prophesying the downfall of the gods even if he does not return the Ring: "All that exists must come to an end. A day of gloom dawns for the gods: again I charge you to give up the Ring!"

Downfall of the gods

Wotan responds thoughtfully to Erda's grave, mysterious and enigmatic pronouncement. As he moves desperately toward her to learn more, the bluish light fades. As she slowly disappears she utters a final message to the confounded god: "I have warned you; you have learned enough; brood now with care and with fear." Wotan turns to anxiety as he ponders thoughtfully and profoundly on Erda's last words.

Fearful, Wotan decides to heed Erda's advice. He becomes overcome by a bold sense of resolution, turns to the Giants while brandishing his Spear, and then hurls the Ring upon the Hoard. Freia, now rescued, runs to the gods who embrace her in relief.

As Fafner begins to pack the Hoard into an enormous sack, the Giants begin to quarrel over their treasure. Fasolt demands equal share of the Hoard, but Fafner reminds his brother that he became foolish and lovesick over Freia, and had to be convinced to exchange her for the Hoard. Besides, if Fasolt had won Freia, would he have shared her with him? As such, Fafner justifies the greater part of the Hoard for himself.

Fasolt appeals to the gods for justice, but Wotan contemptuously turns his back on him. Sarcastically, Loge counsels Fasolt to surrender the treasure, but be sure to take the Ring.

Fasolt assaults Fafner and insists that the Ring belongs to him as compensation for Freia. The Giants struggle for the Ring, each seizing it in turn. Finally, Fafner knocks Fasolt to the ground with a blow from his staff, and then wrenches the Ring from his dying brother's hand. The first materialization of Alberich's curse becomes realized. After Fafner places the Ring on his own finger, he proceeds to quietly pack the remainder of the Hoard. The gods stand in horrified silence, astonished that Alberich's Curse has struck so quickly. Fafner completes the packing of the entire Hoard and departs with the great sack on his back.

Cynically, Loge congratulates Wotan on his incomparable good fortune: he had great luck when he seized the Ring from Alberich, but he has greater fortune now that he has ceded it, for the all-powerful Ring and its Curse will bring misery and death.

Fricka approaches Wotan cajolingly, asking him why he does not enter the noble fortress that awaits him, but Wotan is overcome by a profound sense of guilt, fully realizing that he freed Freia by acquiring her ransom through evil and deceitful actions. Wotan fears the consequences of his actions and resolves that he must soon consult Erda for her wisdom.

Donner ascends a high rock and swings his hammer against it to invoke the elements.

Donner: The Hammer

He - da!   He-da! He-do!   Zu mir, du Ge - düft!

Donner's crashing hammer evokes a blinding flash of lightning that bursts from the clouds, followed by a violent thunderclap. In the gleaming sunlight a great rainbow appears, extending as a bridge from the mountain top to enable the gods to enter Valhalla.

Rainbow Bridge

The gods gaze admiringly at the awesome sight of their new fortress. All proceed toward the rainbow bridge except Loge, who cynically and nonchalantly comments that the gods are hastening toward their doom; he is ashamed of their deceit and duplicity, and no longer wants to share their activities. He prefers to remain behind and transform himself once more into an elemental and wayward flickering fire.

From the depths of the Rhine valley below, the haunting voices of the Rhinemaidens are heard. Their poignant laments call for the return of their Gold and disturb Wotan, who inquires whose plaints he hears. Loge tells him that the children of the Rhine are lamenting their stolen Gold, provoking Wotan to curse them for annoying him in his moment of glory. Loge calls down to the Rhine and delivers the message that it is not Wotan's Will to recover their Gold, but rather, that they should share in this moment of the godhead's glory. As Wotan begins to pass over the bridge, the Rhinemaidens break into a more poignant lament, condemning those on earth as false and contemptible.

The gods cross the rainbow bridge and gloriously enter their new fortress, seemingly confident that their power will remain secure, and with no thought of the inevitable consequences of their failure of conscience. Freia has been rescued, but the all-powerful Ring, Hoard, and Tarnhelm are now in Fafner's possession, jeopardizing the peace of the world.

Wotan knows that he himself cannot wrest the Hoard from Fafner, because that would represent a fatal violation of the Laws etched on his Spear. His thoughts become preoccupied with the idea of creating a surrogate who will act on behalf of the gods, a hero independent of the gods' Will, who will rescue the treasures from Fafner.

Wotan's thoughts then turn to creating a powerful Sword, a divine weapon that will possess magical powers, a Sword that will arm a future hero who will defeat Fafner, recapture the Ring and the treasures, and return the Ring to its primal innocence in the waters of the Rhine, thereby redeeming the world from its present evil by purifying the Ring from Alberich's Curse.

Sword

Libretto

Prelude — Scene 1   **Page 49**

Scene 2   **Page 60**

Scene 3   **Page 75**

Scene 4   **Page 85**

Prelude — Scene 1

The gloomy depths of the Rhine.
Calm waters cover wild configurations of jagged rocks and deep fissures.
Woglinde with her Rinemaiden sisters,
Wellgunde and Flosshilde, swim about playfully.

Woglinde:
Weia! Waga! Woge, du Welle,
walle zur Wiege! Wagala weia!
wallala, weiala weia!

Woglinde:
Weia! Waga! Wandering waters,
swing about in our cradle! Wagala weia!
Walala, weiala weia!

Wellgunde:
Woglinde, wach'st du allein?

Wellgunde: *(from above)*
Woglinde, be careful swimming alone?

Woglinde:
Mit Wellgunde wär' ich zu zwei.

Woglinde:
If Wellgunde joined me, we would be two.

Wellgunde:
Lass' seh'n, wie du wach'st!

Wellgunde:
How safe is it here?

Woglinde:
Sicher vor dir!

Woglinde: *(eludes her by swimming away)*
Safe from your cunning!

Flosshilde:
Heiaha weia! Wildes Geschwister!

Flosshilde: *(from above)*
Heiaha weia! Heedless sprightly caretakers!

Wellgunde:
Flosshilde, schwimm'! Woglinde flieht:
hilf mir die Fließende fangen!

Wellgunde:
Swim Flosshilde! Woglinde is escaping!
Help me catch her!

Flosshilde:
Des Goldes Schlaf hütet ihr schlecht!
Besser bewacht des schlummernden Bett,
sonst büßt ihr beide das Spiel!

Flosshilde:
The sleeping gold is poorly guarded!
Cover the slumberer's bed,
or both of you will repent your sporting!

The Rhinemaidens swim about merrily,
darting about between the rocks.
From a dark chasm, Alberich climbs onto one of the rocks
and observes the water-maidens with increasing pleasure.

Alberich:
Hehe! Ihr Nicker!
Wie seid ihr niedlich, neidliches Volk!
aus Nibelheims Nacht naht' ich mich gern,
neigtet ihr euch zu mir!

Alberich:
Hehe, you nymphs!
You dainty folks delight me!
I come from Nibelheim's darkness;
I'd gladly join you and share your pleasures!

Woglinde:
Hei! Wer ist dort?

Wellgunde:
Es dämmert und ruft!

Flosshilde:
Lugt wer uns belauscht!

Woglinde, Wellgunde:
Pfui! Der Garstige!

Flosshilde:
Hütet das Gold!
Vater warnte vor solchem Feind.

Alberich:
Ihr, da oben!

Rheintöchter:
Was willst du dort unten?

Alberich:
Stör' ich eu'r Spiel,
wenn staunend ich still hier steh'?
tauchtet ihr nieder, mit euch
tollte und neckte der Niblung sich gern.

Woglinde:
Mit uns will er spielen?

Wellgunde:
Ist ihm das Spott?

Alberich:
Wie scheint im Schimmer ihr hell und
schön!
Wie gern umschlänge der Schlanken eine
mein Arm,
schlüpfte hold sie herab!

Flosshilde:
Nun lach' ich der Furcht:
der Feind ist verliebt!

Wellgunde:
Der lüsterne Kauz!

Woglinde:
Hei! Who is there?

Wellgunde:
A voice in the dark!

Flosshilde:
See who is spying on us!

Woglinde, Wellgunde:
What a frightful looking character!

Flosshilde: *(warning the Rhinemaidens)*
Keep an eye on the gold!
Father warned us: watch out for such fiends.

Alberich:
You, above there!

Rhine Daughters:
What do you want down there?

Alberich:
Do I spoil your sport
if I stand here and gaze?
Dive a litle deeper, so this Nibelung can
play with you.

Woglinde:
Does he want to be our playmate?

Wellgunde:
Or does he want to make fun of us?

Alberich:
How bright and fair you are, shining in the
light!
What a pleasure it would be
to hold one of you maidens in my arms;
if she would only come over here?

Flosshilde:
I laugh at being afraid,
but this fiend is in love!

Wellgunde:
What a lascivious beast!

Woglinde:
Laßt ihn uns kennen!

Alberich:
Die neigt sich herab.

Woglinde:
Nun nahe dich mir!

Alberich:
Garstig glatter glitsch'riger Glimmer!
wie gleit' ich aus!
Mit Händen und Füßen nicht fasse noch
halt' ich
das schlecke Geschlüpfer!
Feuchtes Naß füllt mir die Nase:
verfluchtes Niessen!

Woglinde:
Pruhstend naht meines Freiers Pracht!

Alberich:
Mein Friedel sei, du fräuliches Kind!

Woglinde:
Willst du mich frei'n, so freie mich hier!

Alberich:
O weh! Du entweich'st?
Komm doch wieder!
Schwer ward mir, was so leicht du erschwingst.

Woglinde:
Steig' nur zu Grund,
da greifst du mich sicher.

Alberich:
Wohl besser da unten!

Woglinde:
Nun aber nach Oben!

Wellgunde, Flosshilde:
Ha ha ha ha ha ha!

Woglinde:
Let's get closer to him!

Alberich:
One is swimming down to me.

Woglinde:
Come here, closer to me!

Alberich: *(hurriedly)*
Loathsome, slimy pebbles!
I'm slipping on these rocks!
I can't grip anything
with my hands or my feet.
It's treacherous here!
Water is filling my nostrils,
and I can't stop sneezing!

Woglinde: *(laughing at Alberich)*
My wooer comes sputtering!

Alberich: *(trying to embrace Woglinde)*
Fairest child, be mine!

Woglinde: *(avoiding him)*
You want to woo me? Then woo me up there!

Alberich:
You've escaped from me!
Come back!
You can swim where I can scarcely creep.

Woglinde:
Climb to the bottom,
then you'll catch me.

Alberich: *(slides down quickly)*
It's much better down lower!

Woglinde:
Let's go higher!

Wellgunde, Flosshilde:
Ha ha ha ha ha ha!

Alberich:
Wie fang' ich im Sprung den spröden Fisch?
Warte, du Falsche!

Wellgunde:
Heia, du Holder! Hörst du mich nicht?

Alberich:
Rufst du nach mir?

Wellgunde:
Ich rathe dir wohl: zu mir wende dich,
Woglinde meide!

Alberich:
Viel schöner bist du als jene Scheue,
die minder gleißend und gar zu glatt.
Nur tiefer tauche, willst du mir taugen.

Wellgunde:
Bin nun ich dir nah'?

Alberich:
Noch nicht genug!
Die schlanken Arme schlinge um mich,
daß ich den Nacken dir neckend betaste,
mit schmeichelnder Brunst an die
schwellende Brust mich dir schmiege.

Wellgunde:
Bist du verliebt
und lüstern nach Minne,
lass' seh'n, du Schöner, wie bist du zu
schau'n?
Pfui! Du haariger, höckriger Geck!
Schwarzes, schwieliges Schwefelgezwerg!
Such dir ein Friedel, dem du gefällst!

Alberich:
Gefall' ich dir nicht,
dich fass' ich doch fest!

Wellgunde:
Nur fest, sonst fließ' ich dir fort!

Woglinde, Flosshilde:
Ha ha ha ha ha ha!

Alberich:
How can I catch this timid fish?
Wait a while, false one!

Wellgunde:
Hey there, fair one! Don't you hear me?

Alberich: *(turning around)*
Did you call me?

Wellgunde:
I advise you well: come to me
since Woglinde has no interest in you!

Alberich:
You seem far fairer than that shy one,
who looks too sleek.
Dive deeper, if you want to delight me.

Wellgunde:
Now, am I close enough to you?

Alberich:
Not close enough!
Throw your slender arms around me,
so I may touch you and toy with your neck;
and let the heat of my passion press your
soft bosom!

Wellgunde:
Are you bewitched and longing for the joys
of love?
Then show me, handsome,
what favor you have to offer!
How ugly! What a hairy, hideous imp!
A swarthy, spotted, sulphury dwarf!
Do you actually expect to please a lover?

Alberich:
I keep losing my footing,
but my hands can hold you tightly!

Wellgunde: *(quickly swimming away)*
I slipped though your hands!

Woglinde, Flosshilde:
Ha ha ha ha ha ha!

Alberich:
Falsches Kind! Kalter, grätiger Fisch!
Schein' ich nicht schön dir,
niedlich und neckisch, glatt und glau, hei!
So buhle mit Aalen,
ist dir eklig mein Balg!

Flosshilde:
Was zankst du, Alp?
Schon so verzagt?
Du freitest um zwei: früg'st du die Dritte
süßen Trost schüfe die Traute dir!

Alberich:
Holder Sang singt zu mir her!
Wie gut, daß ihr eine nicht seid:
von vielen gefall' ich wohl einer:
bei einer kies'te mich Keine!
Soll ich dir glauben, so gleite herab!

Flosshilde:
Wie thörig seid ihr, dumme Schwestern,
dünkt euch dieser nicht schön!

Alberich:
Für dumm und häßlich darf ich sie halten,
seit ich dich holdeste seh'.

Flosshilde:
O singe fort so süß und fein, wie hehr
verführt es mein Ohr!

Alberich:
Mir zagt, zuckt und zehrt sich das Herz,
lacht mir so zierliches Lob.

Flosshilde:
Wie deine Anmuth mein Aug' erfreut,
deines Lächelns Milde den Muth mir labt!
Seligster Mann!

Alberich:
Süßeste Maid!

Flosshilde:
Wärst du mir hold!

Alberich: *(angrily calling after Wellgunde)*
Faithless thing! Bony, frigid fish!
It seems that I'm not handsome,
pretty and playful, or frisky and bright?
Yes! If I'm so loathsome to you,
then go and flirt with the eels!

Flosshilde:
Why are you such a childish elf?
Why do you suddenly become so sad?
You failed to woo us twice. Perhaps the
sweetness of the third, will bring you love.

Alberich:
What soothing music comes to my ears!
How fortunate that there are more of you.
Yet, one day a maiden may yet choose
and win me.
If you trust me, glide down here!

Flosshilde:
How foolish my senseless sisters are that
they don't find him handsome?

Alberich: *(quickly approaching her)*
I may deem both the others dull and hideous,
but I find you the fairest of all!

Flosshilde:
Sing a sweet song to me;
its charm enraptures my ears!

Alberich: *(confidently caressing her)*
My heart pounds and flutters; it burns
when I hear such sweet praise.

Flosshilde: *(gently resisting him)*
Your sweetness appeals to my eyes,
and your tender smile enlightens my spirit!
Dearest of men!

Alberich:
Sweetest of maidens!

Flosshilde:
If you were only mine!

Alberich:
Hielt' ich dich immer!

Flosshilde:
Deinen stechenden Blick,
deinen struppigen Bart,
o säh' ich ihn, faßt' ich ihn stets!

Deines stachligen Haares
strammes Gelock,
umflöß' es Flosshilde ewig!

Deine Krötengestalt,
deiner Stimme Gekrächz',
o dürft' ich staunend und stumm
sie nur hören und seh'n!

Woglinde, Wellgunde:
Ha ha ha ha ha ha!

Alberich:
Lacht ihr Bösen mich aus?

Flosshilde:
Wie billig am Ende vom Lied!

Woglinde, Wellgunde:
Ha ha ha ha ha ha!

Alberich:
Wehe! ach wehe! O Schmerz! O Schmerz!
Die dritte, so traut, betrog sie mich auch?
Ihr schmählich schlaues, lüderlich schlechtes
Gelichter!
Nährt ihr nur Trug, ihr treuloses
Nickergezücht?

Rheintöchter:
Wallala! Wallala!
Lalaleia! Leialalei! Hheia! Heia! Ha ha!
Schäme dich, Albe!
Schilt nicht dort unten!

Höre was wir dich heißen!
Warum, du Banger, bandest du nicht
das Mädchen, das du minn'st?

Alberich:
If I could only hold you!

Flosshilde: *(ardently)*
The sting of your glance
and the bristle of your beard;
if I could only see and feel forever!

Might the locks of your hair,
so wiry and sharp,
float around Flosshilde forever!

I want to see nothing else,
but your toad-like shape,
or be bedazzled and dumbed,
by the croak of your voice!

Woglinde, Wellgunde:
Ha ha ha ha ha ha!

Alberich: *(startled and alarmed)*
You wretches! Why do you laugh at me?

Flosshilde: *(suddenly darting away)*
A fitting end of the song!

Woglinde, Wellgunde:
Ha ha ha ha ha ha!

Alberich: *(in a wailing voice)*
Woe is me! Ah, woe is me! Alas! Alas!
The third one also betrays me?
You shameless, shifting,
worthless and infamous wantons!
You feed on lies, you treacherous watery
creatures?

Rhine Daughters:
Wallala! Wallala!
lalaleia! leialalei! heia! heia! ha ha!
Shame on you, imp!
Why do you roam about like a child?

Heed the words we tell you!
Why is your heart faint?
Why did you let the maiden go?

Treu sind wir, und ohne Trug
dem Freier, der uns fängt.

We are faithful to the man who can hold us;
and we are free from guile.

Greife nur zu, und grause dich nicht,
in der Fluth entflieh'n wir nicht leicht:
Wallala! lalaleia! leialalei! heia! heia! ha hei!

We gaily work,
and we are fearless in these waters:
Wallala! lalaleia! leialalei! heia! heia! ha hei!

The Rhinemaidens tease Alberich to chase them:
here, there, deeper, apart, and then higher.

Alberich:
Wie in den Gliedern brünstige Gluth mir
brennt und glüht!

Alberich:
A passionate fire inflames my entire body!

Wuth und Minne, wild und mächtig,
wühlt mir den Muth auf!

Fierce rage and longing
overcomes me with madness!

Wie ihr auch lacht und lügt,
lüstern lechz' ich nach euch,
und eine muß mir erliegen!

Though you may laugh at me,
my heart has surrendered to you,
and one of you shall yield to me!

Alberich proceeds to chase the Rhinemaidens with all-consuming desperation.
He climbs the rocks, springs from one to the other; he tries to first catch one,
and then another — they always elude him with mocking laughter.
He staggers and falls into the abyss, then climbs and crawls out and renews the chase.
He almost reaches them, but falls back again, still unable to catch them.
Breathless and enraged, he pauses and raises his clenched fist toward the maidens.

Alberich:
Fing' eine diese Faust!

Alberich:
If I could but capture just one of them!

While in a speechless rage, he gazes upward, when suddenly he is attracted by a spectacle:
through the water above there is a brightening glow, which kindles to a blinding, brightly
shining gleam: a magical light that streams through the water.

Woglinde:
Lugt, Schwestern!
Die Weckerin lacht in den Grund.

Woglinde:
Look, sisters!
The "waking sun" smiles at us in the deep.

Wellgunde:
Durch den grünen Schwall den wonnigen
Schläfer sie grüßt.

Wellgunde:
The radiant sleeper greets us through the
green waters.

Flosshilde:
Jetzt küßt sie sein Auge, daß er es öffne.

Flosshilde:
Now kissing her eyes so as to open them.

Wellgunde:
Schaut', er lächelt in lichtem Schein.

Wellgunde:
Look, smiling in the shining light.

Woglinde:
Durch die Fluthen hin fließt sein strahlender
Stern!

Woglinde:
The glittering rays flow through the
surrounding waters!

Rheintöchter:
Heia jaheia! heia jaheia!
Wallala la la la leia jahei!
Rheingold! Rheingold! Leuchtende Lust,
wie lach'st du so hell und hehr!
Glühender Glanz entgleißet dir weihlich im Wag!

Rhine Daughters: *(praising the Gold)*
Heia jaheia! Heia jaheia!
Wallala la la la leia jahei!
Rhinegold, Rhinegold! Radiant joy:
your gleaming glow
spreads a glorious light over the waves!

Heia jahei! Heia jaheia!
Wache, Freund! Wache froh!
Wonnige Spiele spenden wir dir:
flimmert der Fluß, flammet die Fluth,
umfließen wir tauchend, tanzend und
singend im seligem Bade dein Bett!

Heia jahei! Heia jaheia!
Awake friend! Awake to joy!
We will gladly play with you:
the flashing river, and its flaming waters;
we swim around your bed,
dancing and singing!

Rheingold! Rheingold!
Heia jaheia! Heia jaheia!
Wallala la la la heia jahei!

Rhinegold! Rhinegold!
Heia jaheia! Heia jaheia!
Wallala la la la heia jahei!

The Rhinemaidens swim around the rock with ever-increasing cheerfulness;
the waters surrounding the rock gleam with a golden light.

Alberich:
Was ist's, ihr Glatten, das dort so glänzt
und gleißt?

Alberich: *(his eyes fixed on the Gold)*
What is it, sleek ones, that glows and
glistens over there?

Rheintöchter:
Wo bist du Rauher denn heim, daß vom
Rheingold nie du gehört?

Rhine Daughters
Where have you been that you never heard
of the glorious Rhinegold?

Wellgunde:
Nichts weiß der Alp von des Goldes Auge,
das wechselnd wacht und schläft?

Wellgunde:
The elf knows not of the Gold's brightness:
at times it is awake, and at times asleep?

Woglinde:
Von der Wassertiefe wonnigem Stern,
der hehr die Wogen durchhellt?

Woglinde:
It is the wondrous star of the watery deep,
whose glory shines through the waves?

Rheintöchter:
Sieh, wie selig im Glanze wir gleiten!
Willst du Banger in ihm dich baden,
so schwimm' und schwelge mit uns!
Wallala la la leia lalai!

Rhine Daughters:
See how blithely we glide in its radiance!
Come faint-hearted one, float and frolic
with us; bathe and swim in its glow!
Wallala la la leia jahei!

Alberich:
Eurem Taucherspiele nur taugte das Gold?
Mir gält' es dann wenig!

Woglinde:
Des Goldes Schmuck schmäh'te er nicht,
wüßte er all seine Wunder.

Wellgunde:
Der Welt Erbe gewänne zu eigen,
wer aus dem Rheingold schüfe den Ring,
der maaßlose Macht ihm verlieh'.

Flosshilde:
Der Vater sagt' es, und uns befahl er,
klug zu hüten den klaren Hort,
daß kein Falscher der Fluth ihn entführe:
drum schweigt, ihr schwatzendes Heer!

Wellgunde:
Du klügste Schwester, verklag'st du uns
wohl? Weißt du denn nicht, wem nur allein
das Gold zu schmieden vergönnt?

Woglinde:
Nur wer der Minne Macht entsagt,
nur wer der Liebe Lust verjagt,
nur der erzielt sich den Zauber,
zum Reif zu zwingen das Gold.

Wellgunde:
Wohl sicher sind wir und sorgenfrei,
denn was nur lebt, will lieben,
meiden will keiner die Minne.

Woglinde:
Am wenigsten er, der lüsterne Alp;
vor Liebesgier möcht er vergeh'n!

Flosshilde:
Nicht fürcht' ich den, wie ich ihn erfand:
seiner Minne Brunst brannte fast mich.

Wellgunde:
Ein Schwefelbrand in der Wogen Schwall:
vor Zorn der Liebe zischt er laut!

Alberich:
Is the Gold only for your water games?
That doesn't excite me!

Woglinde:
He wouldn't flaunt the Gold's splendors if
he knew of its wonders.

Wellgunde:
The world's wealth can be won by the man
who fashions a Ring from the Rhinegold;
it would endow him with infinite power!

Flosshilde:
Our father warned us
to guard the shining Hoard wisely,
so that a cunning deceiver
could not steal it!

Wellgunde:
Most prudent sister, why so much caution?
You well know, that there is but one way to
master the power of the Gold?

Woglinde:
Only he who forswears love,
or abstains from the delights of love,
can master the Ring's power
after forging the Gold.

Wellgunde:
We are secure and free from concern,
for all the living craves love;
no one would reject love.

Woglinde:
And least of all, this lascivious dwarf
who could die from his desire to love.

Flosshilde:
I don't fear the elf, whose fiery passion
almost burned me.

Wellgunde:
The lover's frenzy sizzled loudly
as he expressed his passion!

Rheintöchter:
Wallala! Wallaleia la la!
Lieblichster Albe! Lach'st du nicht auch?
In des Goldes Scheine wie leuchtest du schön!
O komm', lieblicher, lache mit uns!
Heia jaheia! Heia jaheia!
Wallala la la la leia jahei!

Rhine Daughters:
Wallala! Wallaleia la la!
Loveliest Niblung! Why not smile?
How fair you are in the Gold's glow!
Come, lovely one, rejoice with us!
Heia jaheia! Heia jaheia!
Wallala la la la leia jahei!

They Rhinemaidens laugh and swim back and forth in the light of the Gold. Alberich keeps his eyes fixed on the Gold, all the while listening to the sisters' chatter.

Alberich:
Der Welt Erbe gewänn' ich zu eigen
durch dich?
Erzwäng' ich nicht Liebe,
doch listig erzwäng' ich mir Lust?
Spottet nur zu!
Der Niblung naht eurem Spiel!

Alberich:
Could I possibly win the world's wealth
through you?
If love shall be denied to me,
my cunning can win another delight?
Keep mocking me!
The Niblung approaches your toy!

Alberich springs to the middle rock and climbs with terrible haste to its summit. The Rhinemaidens separate, shrieking as they swim upward.

Rheintöchter:
Heia! Heia! Heia jahei!
Rettet euch! Es raset der Alp:
in den Wassern sprüht's, wohin er springt:
die Minne macht ihn verrückt!
Ha ha ha ha ha ha ha!

Rhine Daughters:
Heia! Heia! Heia jahei!
Save yourselves! The elf is distraught;
the water swirls wildly wherever he swims:
he has lost his mind for love!
Ha ha ha ha ha ha ha!

Alberich:
Bangt euch noch nicht?
So buhlt nun im Finstern, feuchtes Gezücht!

Alberich: *(springs to the summit)*
You don't fear me yet?
Then frolic in the darkness, watery brood!

Das Licht lösch ich euch aus,
entreiße dem Riff das Gold,
schmiede den rachenden Ring;
denn hör' es die Fluth:
so verfluch' ich die Liebe!

My hand quenches your light,
and then I'll wrest the Gold,
and forge the Ring in revenge;
hear me waves:
henceforth, love shall be accursed!

Alberich rips the gold from the rock, and then plunges with it into the depths, where he quickly disappears. The Rhinemaidens dive down, chasing the robber.

Flosshilde:
Haltet den Räuber!

Flosshilde:
Seize the thief!

Wellgunde:
Rettet das Gold!

Wellgunde:
Rescue the Gold!

Rheintöchter:
Hülfe! Hülfe! Weh'! Weh'!

Rhine Daughters:
Help us! Help us! Woe! Woe!

From the lowest depth, Alberich's shrill mocking laughter is heard.
The rocks disappear into darkness; the waves gradually transform into clouds,
which slowly disperse into a fine mist.
Through small clouds and the mist, an open space on a mountain height becomes visible.
Wotan with Fricka are sleep on a flowery bank.

Scene 2

An open space on a mountain height. As the day dawns,
a castle with glittering pinnacles stands atop a cliff, in the background,
The Rhine flows through a deep valley.
Wotan and Fricka are asleep.

After Fricka awakens, her gaze falls on the castle, now quite visible.

Fricka:
Wotan, Gemahl! Erwache!

Fricka: *(seemingly alarmed)*
Wotan, awaken! Listen!

Wotan:
Der Wonne seligen Saal
bewachen mir Thür und Thor:
Mannes-Ehre, ewige Macht,
ragen zu endlosem Ruhm!

Wotan: *(dreaming)*
A gate and door
guard this sacred dwelling.
Its honor and eternal power
extend our endless renown!

Fricka:
Auf, aus der Träume wonnigem Trug!
Erwache, Mann, und erwäge!

Fricka: *(shakes him)*
Awake from your blissful dreams and
deceit! Awake, and contemplate it!

Wotan:
Vollendet das ewige Werk!
Auf Berges Gipfel die Götterburg;
prächtig prahlt der prangende Bau!

Wie im Traum ich ihn trug,
wie mein Wille ihn wies,
stark und schön steht er zur Schau:
hehrer, herrlicher Bau!

Wotan:
The holy work has been achieved!
On the mountain's summit
the gods' stronghold stands proudly!

My dreams desired it;
my will decreed it,
it stands strong and fair:
a sublime, superb structure!

Fricka:
Nur Wonne schafft dir, was mich
erschreckt? Dich freut die Burg, mir bangt
es um Freia! Achtloser, lass' dich erinnern
des ausbedungenen Lohn's!
Die Burg ist fertig, verfallen das Pfand:
vergaßest du, was du vergab'st?

Fricka:
Your pleasure brings me fear!
You have joy, but I fear for Freia!
Do you remember the reckless promise you
made?
The work is finished. Did you forget the
promise you made to pay for it?

Wotan:
Wohl dünkt mich's, was sie bedungen,
die dort die Burg mir gebaut;
durch Vertrag zähmt ich ihr trotzig Gezücht,
daß sie die hehre Halle mir schüfen;
die steht nun—Dank den Starken:
um den Sold sorge dich nicht.

Wotan:
I well recall the terms for its construction.
I tamed that insolent race
into building this sublime abode,
which stands here
as a tribute to our power.
Pay no heed to its cost!

Fricka:
O lachend frevelnder Leichtsinn!
liebelosester Frohmuth!
Wußt' ich um euren Vertrag, dem Truge
hätt' ich gewehrt; doch muthig entferntet ihr
Männer die Frauen, um taub und ruhig vor
uns, allein mit den Riesen zu tagen:
so ohne Scham verschenktet ihr Frechen
Freia, mein holdes Geschwister,
froh des Schächergewerb's!
Was ist euch Harten doch heilig und werth,
giert ihr Männer nach Macht!

Wotan:
Gleiche Gier war Fricka wohl fremd,
als selbst um den Bau sie mich bat?

Fricka:
Um des Gatten Treue besorgt,
muß traurig ich wohl sinnen,
wie an mich er zu fesseln,
zieht's in die Ferne ihn fort:
herrliche Wohnung, wonniger Hausrath,
sollten dich binden zu säumender Rast.
Doch du bei dem Wohnbau sann'st
auf Wehr und Wall allein:
Herrschaft und Macht soll er dir mehren;
nur rastloser'n Sturm zu erregen,
erstand dir die ragende Burg.

Wotan:
Wolltest du Frau
in der Feste mich fangen,
mir Gotte mußt du schon gönnen,
daß in der Burg gefangen,
ich mir von außen gewinne die Welt:
Wandel und Wechsel liebt wer lebt;
das Spiel drum kann ich nicht sparen!

Fricka:
Liebeloser, leidigster Mann!
Um der Macht und Herrschaft müßigen
Tand verspielst du in lästerndem Spott
Liebe und Weibes Werth?

Fricka:
What impious laughter!
What loveless, cold-hearted folly!
Had I known of your trickery,
I would have prevented the deceit,
but you kept the women away
so you could be alone
when you dealt with the Giants.
You shamelessly and brazenly
bartered Freia, my lovely sister.
With your thirst for power,
nothing is sacred!

Wotan: *(quietly)*
Was Fricka free from greed when she herself
begged me for the building?

Fricka:
It was my concern for my husband's
constancy that made me ponder
how to keep him near me.
When you become tempted to roam,
this stately dwelling might bind you here.
But you were only concerned with glory
and war, so that you could increase your
dominion and power.
These towering walls arose
only to quell the storms
of your unrestrained anxiety.

Wotan: *(smiling)*
You have wanted to confine me
here in the fortress. But I am a God,
and I cannot be imprisoned in a castle.
I must be free to roam
and influence the outside world:
I cannot forego the sport of relinquishing
the game of life and love!

Fricka:
What a cold, unloving, pitiless soul!
For the vain delights of power and
dominion, you insolently scorn
love and a woman's honor?

Wotan:
Um dich zum Weib zu gewinnen,
mein eines Auge setzt' ich werbend daran:
wie thörig tadelst du jetzt!
Ehr' ich die Frauen doch mehr als dich freut;
und Freia, die gute, geb' ich nicht auf;
nie sann dies ernstlich mein Sinn.

Wotan:
When I sought you for a wife,
I sacrificed one of my eyes to win you.
Your scolding is so stupid!
I worship and prize women, and I would
never yield our good Freia. Truthfully,
I never intended to sacrifice the fair one.

Fricka:
So schirme sie jetzt: in schutzloser Angst
läuft sie nach Hilfe dort her.

Fricka: *(looking away, tense and anxious)*
Then protect her now: she is defenseless
and frightened, and hurries here for help.

Freia:
Hilf mir, Schwester! Schütze mich,
Schwäher! Vom Felsen drüben drohte mir
Fasolt, mich Holde käm' er zu holen.

Freia: *(as if in hasty flight)*
Help me, sister! Protect me, brother!
From the other mountain, Fasolt threatens
to abduct me. He's coming here now!

Wotan:
Lass' ihn droh'n! Sah'st du nicht Loge?

Wotan:
Let him threaten! Did you see Loge?

Fricka:
Daß am liebsten du immer dem Listigen
trau'st! Viel Schlimmes schuf er uns schon,
doch stets bestrickt er dich wieder.

Fricka:
You continue to trust that trickster!
He's already done so much harm,
and he continues to want more.

Wotan:
Wo freier Muth frommt,
allein frag' ich nach Keinem.
Doch des Feindes Neid zum Nutz sich
fügen, lehrt nur Schlauheit und List,
wie Loge verschlagen sie übt.
Der zum Vertrage mir rieth,
versprach mir Freia zu lösen:
auf ihn verlass' ich mich nun.

Wotan:
He is my best ally when simple courage is
needed.
Loge artfully employs cunning and guile
to defeat my enemies.
I rely on him;
he advised me to promise Freia
as ransom to the Giants.
I place my faith in him to fix the treaty.

Fricka:
Und er läßt dich allein!
Dort schreiten rasch die Riesen heran:
wo harrt dein schlauer Gehülf'?

Fricka:
And he now forsakes you!
There, the Giants are coming.
Where is your crafty ally?

Freia:
Wo harren meine Brüder,
daß Hülfe sie brächten,
da mein Schwäher die Schwache
verschenkt?
Zu Hülfe, Donner! Hieher, hieher!
Rette Freia, mein Froh!

Freia:
Where are my brothers,
who should be helping me
since my brother-in-law abandons the
weak?
Help me, Donner! Come here!
Froh, come rescue Freia!

Fricka:
Die im bösem Bund dich verriethen,
sie Alle bergen sich nun!

Fricka:
The disgraceful band who betrayed you
have all gone into hiding.

The Giants, Fafner and Fasolt, appear; both are armed with heavy clubs.

Fasolt:
Sanft schloß Schlaf dein Aug';
wir Beide bauten Schlummers baar die Burg.
Mächt'ger Müh' müde nie,
stauten starke Stein' wir auf;
steiler Thurm, Thür' und Thor, deckt und
schließt im schlanken Schloß den Saal.

Fasolt:
You were gently sleeping while we built
your fortress. It was a mighty toil, yet we
untiringly amassing stones that we heaped
high on the lofty tower. A door and gate
guard and enclose the hall of this fine
fortress.

Dort steht's was wir stemmten,
schimmernd hell, bescheint's der Tag;
zieh' nun ein, uns zahl' den Lohn!

There it stands, shining brightly in the
daylight.
Enter, and pay us our wage!

Wotan:
Nennt, Leute, den Lohn;
was dünkt euch zu bedingen?

Wotan:
Name your fee; and ask what you think it's
worth?

Fasolt:
Bedungen ist, was tauglich uns dünkt:
gemahnt es dich so matt?
Freia, die Holde, Holda, die Freie.
vertragen ist's, sie tragen wir heim.

Fasolt:
Did you forget? We fixed a price that we
thought was fair.
We agreed to take Freia, the fair one,
and Holda, the free one.

Wotan:
Seid ihr bei Trost mit eurem Vertrag?
Denkt auf andren Dank:
Freia ist mir nicht feil!

Wotan: *(quickly)*
Has this contract blinded your wits?
Think of another fee.
I cannot trade Freia!

Fasolt:
Was sagst du? ha!
Sinn'st du Verrath? Verrath am Vertrag?
Die dein Speer birgt, sind sie dir Spiel,
des berathnen Bundes Runen?

Fasolt: *(angry and astonished)*
Ha! What are you saying?
Are you planning to betray us?
Are you betraying our agreement?
Are your Runes now just a game?

Fafner:
Getreu'ster Bruder,
merk'st du Tropf nun Betrug?

Fafner: *(scornfully)*
My trusty brother, you fool, do you now
see their guile?

Fasolt:
Lichtsohn du, leicht gefügter!
Hör' und hüte dich; Verträgen halte Treu'!

Fasolt:
Son of light, light of spirit!
Beware! Keep your bond honest!

Was du bist, bist du nur durch Verträge;
bedungen ist, wohl bedacht deine Macht:
bist weiser du als witzig wir sind,
bandest uns Freie zum Frieden du:
all' deinem Wissen fluch' ich,
fliehe weit deinen Frieden,
weißt du nicht offen, ehrlich und frei
Verträgen zu wahren die Treu'!

You are limited by contracts,
and bound by power.
You have more wisdom than we have wits.
You have bound us as freemen to swear that
we keep the peace.
I curse your wisdom
and flee from your peace if you openly
break your faith in our agreement.

Ein dummer Riese räth dir das:
Du Weiser, wiss' es von ihm!

A foolish Giant advises you:
be wise and weigh your words.

Wotan:
Wie schlau für Ernst du achtest,
was wir zum Scherz nur beschlossen!
Die liebliche Göttin, licht und leicht,
was taugt euch Tölpeln ihr Reiz?

Wotan:
How cunning to take seriously
what we only agreed to as a joke!
Of what use is the lovely goddess to
dullards like you?

Fasolt:
Höhn'st du uns? Ha, wie unrecht!
Die ihr durch Schönheit herrscht,
schimmernd hehres Geschlecht,
wir thörig strebt ihr nach
Thürmen von Stein,
setzt um Burg und Saal
Weibes Wonne zum Pfand!

Fasolt:
Are you mocking us? How unjust!
You, hallowed race, rule by radiance and
beauty.
How vain you were in your obsession for
those stone towers,
and you pledged a woman's beauty
for its fortress and hall!

Wir Plumpen plagen uns
schwitzend mit schwieliger Hand,
ein Weib zu gewinnen,
das wonnig und mild
bei uns Armen wohne:
und verkehrt nenn'st du den Kauf?

We dullards have toiled,
with sweat and hardened hands
we toiled to win a gentle woman
to dwell with us.
Do you now betray our pact
and call it a joke?

Fafner:
Schweig' dein faules Schwatzen;
Gewinn werben wir nicht:
Freias Haft hilft wenig doch viel gilt's
den Göttern sie zu entreißen.

Fafner:
Cease your foolish chatter; we gain nothing
from it. Freia's charms serve us little
purpose, but to wrest her from the Gods is
worth much more.

Gold'ne Äpfel wachsen in ihrem Garten,
sie allein weiß die Äpfel zu pflegen;
der Frucht Genuß frommt ihren Sippen
zu ewig nie alternder Jugend:
siech und bleich doch sinkt ihre Blüthe,
alt und schwach schwinden sie hin,
müssen Freia sie missen.
Ihrer Mitte drum sei sie entführt!

Golden apples grow in her garden;
she alone knows how to tend to them!
The fruit endows her kindred
with eternal youth.
If they are forced to forego Freia,
their flowering shall wane;
then they will waste away, old and weak.
So let's take her from their midst!

Wotan:
Loge säumt zu lang'!

Fasolt:
Schlicht gib nun Bescheid!

Wotan:
Fordert andern Sold!

Fasolt:
Kein andrer: Freia allein!

Fafner:
Du da! Folge uns!

Fafner and Fasolt press toward Freia. Froh and Donner appear anxiously.

Freia:
Helft! Helft vor den Harten!

Froh:
Zu mir, Freia!

Meide sie, Frecher!
Froh schützt die Schöne.

Donner:
Fasolt und Fafner, fühltet ihr schon meines
Hammers harten Schlag?

Fafner:
Was soll das Droh'n?

Fasolt:
Was dring'st du her?
Kampf kies'ten wir nicht,
verlangen nur unsern Lohn.

Donner:
Schon oft zahlt ich Riesen den Zoll.
Kommt her, des Lohnes Last
wäg' ich mit gutem Gewicht!

Wotan:
Halt, du Wilder! Nichts durch Gewalt!
Verträge schützt meines Speeres Schaft:
spar' deines Hammers Heft!

Wotan: *(to himself)*
Why is Loge lingering so long!

Fasolt:
Give us a straight answer!

Wotan:
Ask for another fee!

Fasolt:
No other, only Freia!

Fafner:
You, there! follow us!

Freia:
Help! Help me from these ruffians!

Froh: *(clasping Freia in his arms)*
Come to me, Freia!
(to Fafner)
Stay away from her, rascal!
Froh shall protect the fair one!

Donner: *(in front of the two Giants)*
Fasolt and Fafner, you have not yet felt
the weight of my hammer's blow?

Fafner:
Why do you threaten us?

Fasolt:
Why are you rushing us?
We sought no conflict.
We only ask for our wage.

Donner:
I've paid the Giants their due many times.
If you come near, you'll get your due in full
measure!

Wotan: *(holding forth his Spear)*
Hold on, hotheads! Force brings nothing!
My Spear protects bonds,
so spare your hammer's heft!

Freia:
Wehe! Wehe! Wotan verläßt mich!

Fricka:
Begreif' ich dich noch, grausamer Mann?

Wotan:
Endlich Loge!
Eiltest du so, den du geschlossen,
den schlimmen Handel zu schlichten?

Loge:
Wie? Welchen Handel hätt' ich geschlossen?
Wohl was mit den Riesen dort im Rahte du
dang'st?
In Tiefen und Höhen treibt mich mein Hang;
Haus und Herd behagt mir nicht.

Donner und Froh, die denken an Dach und
Fach,
wollen sie frei'n, ein Haus muß sie erfreu'n.
Ein stolzer Saal, ein starkes Schloß,
danach stand Wotans Wunsch.

Haus und Hof, Saal und Schloß,
die selige Burg, sie steht nun fest gebaut.
Das Pracht gemäuer prüft' ich selbst,
ob alles fest, forscht' ich genau;
Fasolt und Fafner fand ich bewährt:
kein Stein wankt im Gestemm.

Nicht müßig war ich, wie mancher hier;
der lügt, wer lässig mich schilt!

Wotan:
Arglistig weich'st du mir aus:
mich zu betrügen hüte in Treuen dich wohl!
Von allen Göttern dein einz'ger Freund,
nahm ich dich auf in der übel trauenden
Troß.

Nun red' und rathe klug!
Da einst die Bauer der Burg
zum Dank Freia bedangen,
du weißt, nicht anders willigt' ich ein,
als weil auf Pflicht du gelobtest
zu lösen das hehre Pfand?

Freia:
Woe's me! Wotan forsakes me!

Fricka:
Is this resolved, merciless man?

Wotan: *(Wotan sees Loge coming)*
At last, Loge is here!
Is this how you rush to mend the evil
contract that you tricked me into?

Loge:
What? What bargain did I make?
Didn't you make the contract with the
Giants?
My whim takes me to depths and heights;
house and hearth do not please me.

Donner and Froh dream of household joys;
if they should wed,
a home would bring them joy.
That was Wotan's wish: a stately home,
that would also be a fortress.

The glorious fortress now stands firmly.
I made sure it was solid;
I tested it myself.
I found Fasolt and Fafner unreliable,
there was not a stone
that was firmly in its place.

I wasn't idle, like many here;
those who rebuke me as lazy, are liars.

Wotan:
You slyly evade the issue?
Beware, if you are betraying my trust!
Of all the Gods, I am your only friend.
I vowed for you after the others mistrusted
you.

Now speak and give us good counsel!
When the builders stipulated
that Freia would be payment,
you know that I agreed
because you promised
to release us from the pledge?

Loge:
Mit höchster Sorge drauf zu sinnen,
wie es zu lösen, das hab' ich gelobt.
Doch, daß ich fände was nie sich fügt, was
nie gelingt, wie ließ' sich das wohl geloben?

Loge:
I promised the utmost care
in determining how to release her.
But how could I succeed,
if no promise had ever been given?

Fricka:
Sieh, welch' trugvollem Schelm du getraut!

Fricka: *(to Wotan)*
See what a traitorous knave you trusted!

Froh:
Loge heißt du, doch nenn' ich dich Lüge!

Froh:
You call yourself Loge, but I call you liar!

Donner:
Verfluchte Lohe, dich lösch' ich aus!

Donner:
Accursed fire, I will quench your glow!

Loge:
Ihre Schmach zu decken schmähen mich
Dumme!

Loge:
The fools revile me so that they can cover
their disgrace!

Wotan:
In Frieden laßt mir den Freund!
Nicht kennt ihr Loges Kunst:
reicher wiegt seines Rathes Werth,
zahlt er zögernd ihn aus.

Wotan: *(steps between them)*
Leave my friend in peace!
If you knew Loge's wiles;
his counsel becomes richer
when he delays in giving it.

Fafner:
Nichts gezögert! rasch gezahlt!

Fafner:
No more delay! Pay up promptly!

Fasolt:
Lang währt's mit dem Lohn!

Fasolt:
We await our wages!

Wotan:
Jetzt hör', Störrischer! Halte Stich!
Wo schweiftest du hin und her?

Wotan: *(turning urgently to Loge)*
Listen, shifty one! Keep your word!
Where have you been straying?

Loge:
Immer ist Undank Loges Lohn! Für dich nur
besorgt, sah ich mich um, durch stöbert im
Sturm alle Winkel der Welt: Ersatz für Freia
zu suchen, wie er den Riesen wohl recht.

Umsonst sucht' ich, und sehe nun wohl:
in der Welten Ring nichts ist so reich,
als Ersatz zu muthen dem Mann für Weibes
Wonne und Werth!

Loge:
Ingratitude has always been my lot!
I searched feverishly, ransacking the ends of
the earth for a substitute for Freia
that would be fair to the Giants.

I searched in vain and found that there is
nothing so rich in this whole wide world
that a man could accept as a substitute for a
woman's beauty and pleasure!

All seem overwhelmed, perplexed as well as amazed.

So weit Leben und Weben, in Wasser, Erd'
und Luft, viel frug' ich, forschte bei allen,
wo Kraft nur sich rührt, und Keime sich
regen: was wohl dem Manne mächt'ger
dünk', als Weibes Wonne und Wert?

I asked all men about life's forces
and its beginnings: about life in water, about
earth and air.
What is more precious to a man
than a woman's and pleasure?

Doch so weit Leben und Weben,
verlacht nur ward meine fragende List:
in Wasser, Erd' und Luft,
lassen will nichts von Lieb' und Weib.

But wherever there was life and being,
my cunning question was derided:
whether on earth, in air or water,
no one would forsake the joy of love

Nur einen sah' ich, der sagte der Liebe ab:
um rothes Gold entrieth er des Weibes Gunst.

But only one renounced a woman's love, a
sacrifice for the shining Gold.

Des Rheines klare Kinder klagten mir ihre
Noth: der Nibelung, Nacht-alberich,
buhlte vergebens um der Badenden Gunst;
das Rheingold da raubte sich rächend der
Dieb: das dünkt ihn nun das theuerste Gut,
hehrer als Weibes Huld.

The Rhine's innocent children bewailed
their plight: the Nibelung, Night-Alberich,
sought the maiden's favors, but in vain.
In revenge, the robber stole the Rhinegold,
and now reveres it as earth's most precious
prize, one greater than a woman's grace.

Um den gleißenden Tand, der Tiefe
entwandt, erklang mir der Töchter Klage:
an dich, Wotan, wenden sie sich,
daß zu Recht du zögest den Räuber,
das Gold dem Wasser wieder gebest,
und ewig es bliebe ihr eigen.

The maidens wept to Wotan,
and prayed that vengeance
would befall the Niblung,
and that the thief would be brought to
justice and return the Gold to the waters, to
glisten there forever.

Dir's zu melden gelobt' ich den Mädchen:
nun lös'te Loge sein Wort.

I kept my faith: I promised the maidens
that I would inform you of this crime!

Wotan:
Thörig bist du, wenn nicht gar tückisch!
Mich selbst siehst du in Noth:
wie hülf' ich andern zum Heil?

Wotan:
You are mad, if not downright malicious!
How can I help others when I find myself
in serious trouble?

Fasolt:
Nicht gönn' ich das Gold dem Alben; viel
Noth schon schuf uns der Niblung; doch
schlau entschlüpfte unserm Zwange immer
der Zwerg.

Fasolt:
I begrudge the Niblung the Gold;
He has already done much harm to us
yet the Dwarf always seems to slyly slip
away from us.

Fafner:
Neue Neidthat sinnt uns der Niblung,
gibt das Gold ihm Macht.

Fafner:
With the Gold's power, the Niblung will
plot new mischief against us.

Du da, Loge! Sag' ohne Lug:
was Großes gilt denn das Gold,
daß dem Niblung es genügt?

Loge:
Ein Tand ist's in des Wassers Tiefe,
lachenden Kindern zur Lust;
doch ward es zum runden Reife
geschmiedet, hilft es zur höchsten Macht,
gewinnt dem Manne die Welt.

Wotan:
Von des Rheines Gold hört ich raunen:
Beuterunen berge sein rother Glanz;
Macht und Schätze schüf' ohne Maaß ein
Reif

Fricka:
Taugte wohl des gold'nen Tandes gleißend
Geschmeid auch Frauen zu schönem Schmuck?

Loge:
Des Gatten Treu' ertrotzte die Frau,
trüge sie hold den hellen Schmuck,
den schimmernd Zwerge schmieden
rührig im Zwange des Reifs.

Fricka:
Gewänne mein Gatte sich wohl das Gold?

Wotan:
Des Reifes zu walten,
räthlich will es mich dünken.
Doch wie, Loge, lernt' ich die Kunst?
wie schüf ich mir das Geschmeid?

Loge:
Ein Runenzauber zwingt das Gold zum
Reif; keiner kennt ihn; doch einer übt ihn
leicht, der sel'ger Lieb' entsagt.

Das spar'st du wohl; zu spät auch käm'st
du; Alberich zauderte nicht.
Zaglos gewann er des Zaubers Macht:
gerathen ist ihm der Ring!

Listen, Loge! Tell me truthfully:
what value is in the Gold that the Niblung
holds so dear?

Loge:
It's a toy in the waters depth providing
pleasure to delight the Rhine children;
but if was fashioned into a Ring,
it would bestow measureless power
and win mastery of the world for its lord.

Wotan: *(thoughtfully)*
I have heard rumors about the Rhinegold:
its glittering glow hides Runes of riches;
a Ring that would provide unbounded
power and wealth.

Fricka: *(softly to Loge)*
Would its glitter also serve to make golden
trinkets to adorn a woman?

Loge:
Hidden in the Ring's thrall, a wife could
ensure her husband's fidelity if she adorned
herself in bright ornaments made from the
Dwarf's forge.

Fricka: *(caressingly to Wotan)*
O, might my husband win the Gold?

Wotan: *(appearing to be under a spell)*
It seems wise to me that we control the
power of the Ring.
But Loge, how can I learn the art of forging
this gem?

Loge:
A magic spell turns the Gold into a Ring.
No one knows it, but by foreswearing
blessed love, anyone can easily acquire it.

That you shall not do; you are too late.
But Alberich did not delay. He boldly
gained the power of the spell, and has now
forged the Ring!

Donner:
Zwang uns allen schüfe der Zwerg,
würd' ihm der Reif nicht entrissen.

Donner: *(to Wotan)*
If the Ring is not wrested from Alberich,
he would enslave us all.

Wotan:
Den Ring muß ich haben!

Wotan:'
I must have the Ring!

Froh:
Leicht erringt ohne Liebesfluch er sich jetzt.

Froh:
It can easily be won, without cursing love.

Loge:
Spottleicht, ohne Kunst, wie im Kinderspiel!

Loge: *(harshly)*
Easy, without skill, like child's play!

Wotan:
So rathe, wie?

Wotan:
Tell us how?

Loge:
Durch Raub!
Was ein Dieb stahl, das stiehl'st du dem
Dieb; ward leichter ein Eigen erlangt?
Doch mit arger Wehr wahrt sich Alberich;
klug und fein mußt du verfahren,
zieh'st den Räuber du zu Recht,
um des Rheines Töchtern, den rothen Tand.
Das Gold wieder zu geben; denn darum
flehen sie dich.

Loge:
By theft!
What a thief stole, steal from the thief:
could possessions more easily be acquired?
Alberich guards it with guile;
you must act shrewdly and subtly in order
to bring the thief to justice, and also return
the Gold to the Rhinemaidens.
They beg you to return the shining Gold to
the Rhine.

Wotan:
Des Rheines Töchter?
Was taugt mir der Rath?

Wotan:
The Rhine daughters?
What does their counsel mean to me?

Fricka:
Von dem Wassergezücht mag ich nichts
wissen; schon manchen Mann mir zum
Leid! verlockten sie buhlend im Bad.

Fricka:
I have no interest in knowing about this
watery brood. To my distress, many a man
has been lured into their watery lair.

Wotan stands silently, struggling within himself. The other Gods fix their eyes on him, in mute suspense. Meanwhile Fafner has been conferring with Fasolt.

Fafner:
Glaub' mir, mehr als Freia frommt das
gleißende Gold: auch ew'ge Jugend erjagt,
wer durch Goldes Zauber sie zwingt.
Hör', Wotan, der Harrenden Wort!
Freia bleib' euch in Frieden; leicht'ren Lohn
fand ich zur Lösung: uns rauhen Riesen
genügt des Niblungen rothes Gold.

Fafner: *(to Fasolt)*
Trust me, the glittering Gold is worth more
than Freia: the one who commands the
Gold's magic gains eternal youth.
Listen, Wotan, we await your word!
Freia may remain with you in peace.
As a better alternative, we Giants would be
content with Nibelheim's Gold as payment.

Wotan:
Seid ihr bei Sinn? Was nicht ich besitze,
soll ich euch Schamlosen schenken?

Wotan:
Have you lost your mind? How can I give
you, shameless ones, what I do not own?

Fafner:
Schwer baute dort sich die Burg:
leicht wird dir's mit list'ger Gewalt
den Niblungen fest zu fah'n.

Fafner:
Hard labor built the fortress, but with your
cunning and power, it should be easy for
you to seize the Niblung Gold.

Wotan:
Für euch müht' ich mich um den Alben?
für euch fing ich den Feind?
Unverschämt und überbegehrlich,
macht euch Dumme mein Dank!

Wotan:
Shall I deal with the Niblung for you?
Should I shackle the foe for you?
You fools! My debt has made you insolent
and greedy!

Fasolt suddenly seizes Freia and draws her to the side with Fafner.

Fafner:
Hieher, Maid! In uns're Macht!
Als Pfand folg'st du uns jetzt,
bis wir Lösung empfah'n!

Fafner:
Come here, girl! You are in our power!
Stay with us as a hostage until your
ransom has been paid!

Freia:
Wehe! Wehe! Weh!

Freia: *(screaming)*
Woe is me! Woe is me! Woe!

Fafner:
Fort von hier sei sie entführt!
Bis Abend, achtet's wohl!
pflegen wir sie als Pfand; wir kehren wieder;
doch kommen wir, und bereit liegt nicht als
Lösung, das Rheingold licht und roth.

Fafner:
Let's carry her far from here!
We'll hold her as hostage till evening!
When we return at night,
the bright gleaming Rhinegold
must be ready for us!

Fasolt:
Zu End' ist die Frist dann,
Freia verfallen: für immer folge sie uns!

Fasolt:
Then the time is up. If not, Freia will be
forfeited and ready to go with us!

Freia:
Schwester! Brüder! Rettet! Helft!

Freia: *(screaming)*
Sister, Brothers! Save me! Help!

Freia is borne away by the hastily retreating Giants.

Froh:
Auf, ihnen nach!

Froh:
Up, after them!

Donner:
Breche denn alles!

Donner:
Break it all up!

Freia:
Rettet! Helft!

Freia: *(in the distance)*
Save me! Help!

Loge:
Über Stock und Stein zu Thal stapfen sie
hin:
durch des Rheines Wasserfurth waten die
Riesen.
Fröhlich nicht hängt Freia
den Rauhen über dem Rücken!
Heia! hei! Wie taumeln die Tölpel dahin!

Durch das Thal talpen sie schon. Wohl an
Riesenheims Mark erst halten sie Rast.

Was sinnt nun Wotan so wild?
Den sel'gen Göttern wie geht's?

Loge: *(gazing at the Giants)*
Over stock and stone they stride down the
valley: the Giants wade through the fjord
and across the Rhine.

Sadly, Freia is there, roughly borne on the
ruffians' shoulders!
Heia! hei! The louts lumber along!

Now they tramp through the valley, and
rest at Riesenheim.

How darkly Wotan broods?
What ails the glorious Gods?

*A pale mist gradually grows more dense. The Gods' appearance
becomes increasingly wan and aged. All look at Wotan, anxiously and in dismay.
Wotan is in deep thought as he stares fixedly at the ground.*

Trügt mich ein Nebel? neckt mich ein
Traum?
Wie bang und bleich verblüht ihr so bald!
Euch erlischt der Wangen Licht;
der Blick eures Auges verblitzt!
Frisch, mein Froh! Noch ist's ja früh!
Deiner Hand, Donner, entsinkt ja der
Hammer!
Was ist's mit Fricka? Freut sie sich wenig
ob Wotans grämlichem Grau,
das schier zum Greisen ihn schafft?

Do the mists trick me? Do they mock my
dream?
How anxious and pale you have suddenly
become!
The bloom has fled your cheeks,
and brightness has faded from your eyes!
Courage, Froh! It is only dawn!
The hammer escapes Donner's hand!
Is Fricka grieving? Is she in sorrow
for Wotan's gloomy, that has suddenly
turned him old and grey!

Fricka:
Wehe! Wehe! Was ist gescheh'n?

Fricka:
What has befallen us?

Donner:
Mir sinkt die Hand!

Donner:
My arm is sinking!

Froh:
Mir stockt das Herz!

Froh:
My heart stands still!

Loge:
Jetzt fand' ich's! hört, was euch fehlt!
Von Freias Frucht genosset ihr heute noch nicht.
Die goldnen Äpfel in ihrem Garten,
sie machten euch tüchtig und jung,
aß't ihr sie jeden Tag.

Loge:
I now see what you lack!
You have not eaten Freia's fruit today.
The golden apples that grow in her garden,
made you hearty and young when you ate
them every day.

Des Gartens Pflegerin ist nun verpfändet;
an den Ästen darbt und dorrt das Obst,
bald fällt faul es herab.

Mich kümmert's minder; an mir ja kargte
Freia von je knausernd die köstliche Frucht:
denn halb so ächt nur bin ich wie, Selige, ihr!

Doch ihr setztet alles auf das jüngende
Obst: das wußten die Riesen wohl;
auf eurer Leben legten sie's an:
nun sorgt, wie ihr das wahrt!

Ohne die Äpfel, alt und grau, greis und
grämlich, welkend zum Spott aller Welt,
erstirbt der Götter Stamm.

Fricka:
Wotan, Gemahl! Unsel'ger Mann!
Sieh, wie dein Leichtsinn lachend uns allen
Schimpf und Schmach erschuf!

Wotan:
Auf, Loge! Hinab mit mir!
Nach Nibelheim fahren wir nieder:
gewinnen will ich das Gold.

Loge:
Die Rheintöchter riefen dich an:
so dürfen Erhörung sie hoffen?

Wotan:
Schweige, Schwätzer! Freia, die Gute,
Freia gilt es zu lösen!

Loge:
Wie du befiehlst, führ' ich dich schnell
steil hinab steigen wir denn durch den Rhein?

Wotan:
Nicht durch den Rhein!

Loge:
So schwingen wir uns durch die
Schwefelkluft. Dort schlüpfe mit mir hinein!

The garden's keeper is now a hostage,
and the fruit fades and withers on the
branches; soon it will decay and die.

It irks me less because Freia has always
been ungenerous with the precious fruit;
but I am half as godlike as you great ones!

You set your fortune on the youth-giving
fruit. The Giants knew your secret;
they set your lives against it,
and now you must carefully defend it

Without apples, you become old and grey,
worn and weary. The race of Gods are the
scorn of the world, and they will soon die.

Fricka: *(anxiously)*
Wotan, my husband! Unhappy man!
See how your thoughtlessness has brought
us shame and disgrace!

Wotan: *(with sudden resolve)*
Come, Loge! Come down with me!
We will descend to Nibelheim;
I will procure the Gold.

Loge:
The Rhinemaidens are calling you:
and they hope you will listen to them?

Wotan: *(violently)*
Be quiet, you babbler!
We must free the fair Freia!

Loge:
At you command, we'll go swiftly,
and travel through the Rhine.

Wotan:
But not through the Rhine!

Loge:
Then we'll swing ourselves down through
the sulfur-cleft! Slip into it with me!

Wotan:
Ihr andern harrt bis Abend hier: verlor'ner
Jugend erjag' ich erlösen des Gold!

Wotan:
You others wait here till evening!
The redeeming Gold will win back our youth!

Wotan follows Loge into the cleft. The sulfurous vapor quickly transforms into thick clouds.

Donner:
Fahre wohl, Wotan!

Donner:
Farewell, Wotan!

Froh:
Glück auf! Glück auf!

Froh:
Good luck! Good luck!

Fricka:
O kehre bald zur bangenden Frau!

Fricka:
Return soon to your sorrowing wife!

The vapor thickens to a rising black cloud. It clears into a dark, rocky chasm.
In the distance, a reddish glow is seen, together with the noise of forging.
After the clanging of anvils diminishes, a subterranean cavern becomes visible,
which opens to narrow shafts and clefts on all sides.

END of SCENE 2

Scene 3

Nibelheim - a subterranean cavern
Alberich drags the shrieking Mime from a shaft.

Alberich:
Hehe! Hehe! Hieher! Hieher!
Tückischer Zwerg!
Tapfer gezwickt, sollst du mir sein,
schaffst du nicht fertig, wie ich's bestellt,
zur Stund' das feine Geschmeid!

Alberich:
Hehe! Hehe! Come here, mischievous
Dwarf!
You'll be unmercifully squashed if you
haven't finished making that finely-wrought
Gold piece that I commanded you to make!

Mime:
Ohe! Ohe! Au! Au!
Lass' mich nur los! Fertig ist's, wie du
befahl'st mit Fleiß und Schweiß ist es
gefügt: nimm' nur die Nägel vom Ohr!

Mime: *(howling)*
Ohe! Ohe! Au! Au!
Let me go! I forged it!
It involved incredible drudgery and hard
work! Take your fingers from my ear!

Alberich:
Was zögerst du dann, und zeigst es nicht?

Alberich:
Why won't you show it to me?

Mime:
Ich Armer zagte, daß noch was fehle.

Mime:
I hesitated lest something might be missing.

Alberich:
Was wär' noch nicht fertig?

Alberich:
When will it be fully completed?

Mime:
Hier, und da.

Mime: *(embarrassed)*
Here, and over there.

Alberich:
Was hier und da? Her das Geschmeid!

Alberich:
What here and there? Give it to me!

Alberich tries to grab his ear. Mime is terrified; he drops a piece of metal work
that he was holding tightly. Alberich picks it up quickly, and examines it carefully.

Schau, du Schelm! Alles geschmiedet
und fertig gefügt, wie ich's befahl!
So wollte der Tropf schlau mich betrügen?
für sich behalten das hehre Geschmeid,
das meine List ihn zu schmieden gelehrt?
Kenn' ich dich dummen Dieb?

See, you scoundrel! All has been forged
as I commanded, finished and ready.
Ah, did this cunning dolt try to deceive me
and keep this wonderful work for himself:
the work I taught him forge?
Have I discovered a stupid thief?

He places the magic Tarnhelm on his head and invokes its spell.

Dem Haupt fügt sich der Helm: ob sich der
Zauber auch zeigt?

The helmet fits.
Will the spell work?

"Nacht und Nebel. Niemand gleich!"   "Night and darkness. No one sees me!"

Alberich's form vanishes; a colum of mist replaces him.

Siehst du mich, Bruder?   Can you see me, brother?

Mime: **Mime:** *(looks about, astonished)*
Wo bist du? Ich sehe dich nicht.   Where are you? I can't see you.

Alberich: **Alberich:** *(invisible)*
So fühle mich doch, du fauler Schuft!   Then feel me instead, you lazy rascal!
Nimm' das für dein Diebsgelüst!   Take that for your thievish thought!

Mime writhes from Alberich's blows.

Mime: **Mime:**
Ohe, Ohe! Au! Au! Au!   Ohe! Ohe! Au! Au! Au!

Alberich: **Alberich:** *(laughing, invisible)*
Ha ha ha ha ha ha!   Ha ha ha ha ha ha!
Hab' Dank, du Dummer!   Thank you, stupid!
Dein Werk bewährt sich gut!   Your work stood the test!
Hoho! Hoho!   Hoho! Hoho!
Niblungen all', neigt euch nun Alberich!   All you Nibelungs, bow down to Alberich!

Überall weilt er nun euch zu bewachen;   He watches you from all over.
Ruh' und Rast ist euch zerronnen;   Peace and rest have ended for you.
ihm müßt ihr schaffen, wo nicht ihr ihn   You must now toil for me,
schaut; wo nicht ihr ihn gewahrt, seid seiner even without seeing me.
gewärtig! Unterthan seid ihr ihm immer!   You are my vassals forever!
Hoho! Hört' ihn, er naht: der Niblungen Herr! Hoho! Hoho! Hear the Nibelungs' lord!

***The misty column of vapor disappears. Alberich's scolding becomes more faint.
Wotan and Loge appear from a cleft in the rock.***

Loge: **Loge:**
Nibelheim hier. Durch bleiche Nebel   Here is Nibelheim. What are those fiery
was blitzen dort feurige Funken?   sparks flashing through the vapors?

Mime: **Mime:** *(in pain)*
Au! Au! Au!   Au! Au! Au!

Wotan: **Wotan:**
Hier stöhnt es laut: was liegt im Gestein?   Those groans! What lies among the rocks?

Loge: **Loge:** *(bends over Mime)*
Was Wunder wimmerst du hier?   Why do you whimper, strange one?

Mime:
Ohe! Ohe! Au! Au!

Loge:
Hei, Mime! Muntrer Zwerg!
Was zwickt und zwackt dich denn so?

Mime:
Laß mich in Frieden!

Loge:
Das will ich freilich, und mehr noch, hör':
helfen will ich dir, Mime!

Mime:
Wer hülfe mir!
Gehorchen muß ich dem leiblichen Bruder,
der mich in Bande gelegt.

Loge:
Dich, Mime, zu binden, was gab ihm die Macht?

Mime:
Mit arger List schuf sich Alberich aus
Rheines Gold einem gelben Reif: seinem
starken Zauber zittern wir staunend; mit
ihm zwingt er uns alle, der Niblungen
nächtges Heer.

Sorglose Schmiede, schufen wir sonst wohl
Schmuck unsern Weibern,
wonnig Geschmeid', niedlichen
Niblungentand; wir lachten lustig der Müh'.

Nun zwingt uns der Schlimme,
in Klüfte zu schlüpfen,
für ihn allein uns immer zu müh'n.

Durch des Ringes Gold erräth seine Gier,
wo neuer Schimmer in Schachten sich birgt:
da müssen wir spähen, spüren und graben,
die Beute schmelzen, und schmieden den
Guß, ohne Ruh' und Rast dem Herrn zu
häufen den Hort.

Loge:
Dich Trägen soeben traf wohl sein Zorn?

Mime:
Ohe! Ohe! Au! Au!

Loge:
It's the merry Dwarf Mime!
Why are you whining?

Mime:
Leave me in peace!

Loge:
I will, and gladly listen to you,
and I also promise to help you!

Mime:
Who can possibly help me?
I must obey the behest of my brother,
who has enslaved me!

Loge:
But what gave him the power to bind you?

Mime:
Alberich applied his evil cunning
to mold the Ring from the Rhinegold!
He has overcome
the Nibelung's laziness
by using its power and magic.

We were once carefree smiths!
We made ornaments and trinkets for our
women; dainty trifles that we lightly
rejoiced with.

Now this wretch compels us
to creep into caverns,
and toil for him alone.

The Ring of Gold inspires his greed.
Where new treasure hides in the clefts,
we must find it and dig for it,
and then melt the booty and forge the Gold.
There is no peace or pause in piling up the
master's hoard.

Loge:
You idleness roused his ire?

Mime:
Mich Ärmsten,
ach, mich zwang er zum Ärgsten:
Ein Helmgeschmeid' hieß er mich chweißen;
genau befahl er, wie es zu fügen.

Wohl merkt' ich klug, welch mächt'ge Kraft
zu eigen dem Werk, das aus Erz ich wob;
für mich drum hüten wollt' ich dem Helm;
durch seinen Zauber Alberichs Zwang mich
entziehn.

Vielleicht, ja vielleicht den Lästigen selbst
überlisten, in meine Gewalt ihn zu werfen;
den Ring ihm zu entreißen, daß, wie ich
Knecht jetzt dem Kühnen, mir Freien er
selber dann fröhn'!

Loge:
Warum, du Kluger, glückte dir's nicht?

Mime:
Ach! Der das Werk ich wirkte,
den Zauber, der ihm entzückt,
den Zauber errieth ich nicht recht!
der das Werk mir rieth, und mir's entriß,
der lehrte mich nun, doch leider zu spät,
welche List läg' in dem Helm:

Meinem Blick entschwand er;
doch Schwielen dem Blinden schlug
unschaubar sein Arm.

Das schuf ich mir Dummen schön zu Dank!

Loge:
Gesteh', nicht leicht gelingt der Fang.

Wotan:
Doch erliegt der Feind, hilft deine List!

Mime:
Mit eurem Gefrage,
wer seid denn ihr Fremde?

Mime:
Poor Mime,
he forced the hardest tasks on me.
He made me forge and weld a helmet; and
gave me exact orders how I was to make it.

I shrewdly noted what mighty power lay in
the work I had fashioned from the metal.
So I wanted to keep the helmet for myself,
and through its spell escape from Alberich's
sway.

Perhaps I could outwit the tyrant myself,
get him into my power,
and snatch the Ring from him.
But now,
I still serve him as his slave!

Loge:
And why, wise one, didn't you succeed?

Mime:
Ah! Though I fashioned the work,
I didn't guess properly
about the magic of its spell.
Alberich planned the work,
but then he seized it, and taught me about
the spell of the helm; it was too late.

What cunning lay in making the Tarnhelm.
He vanished from my sight, unseen as he
exerted his power on me; I was blind.

Such was my reward. What a fool I was!

Loge: *(laughs with Wotan)*
Our task will not be easy!

Wotan:
With your cunning, the foe will fall!

Mime:
Who are you strangers?
What do your questions mean?

Loge:
Freunde dir; von ihrer Noth
befrei'n wir der Niblungen Volk!

Mime:
Nehmt euch in Acht; Alberich naht.

Wotan:
Sein' harren wir hier.

Loge:
We are friends of the Niblungen, and we will
free them from their misery!

Mime: *(shrinks as Alberich approaches)*
Beware, Alberich draws near!

Wotan:
We'll wait here for him.

Alberich appears before them. He removes the Tarnhelm and brandishes a whip.
Nibelungs from the caverns below are laden with Gold and silver handiwork,
which, they heap together in a large pile, under Alberich's continuous scolding.

Alberich:
Hieher! Dorthin! Hehe! Hoho!
Träges Heer! Dort zu Hauf schichtet den
Hort!
Du da, hinauf! Willst du voran?
Schmähliches Volk! Ab das Geschmeide!
Soll ich euch helfen? Alle hieher!

He! Wer ist dort? Wer drang hier ein?
Mime, zu mir! Schäbiger Schuft!
Schwatztest du gar mit
dem schweifenden Paar?
Fort, du Fauler!
Willst du gleich schmieden und schaffen?

He! An die Arbeit!
Alle von hinnen! Hurtig hinab!
Aus den neuen Schachten schafft mir das Gold!
Euch grüßt die Geißel, grabt ihr nicht rasch!

Daß keiner mir müßig, bürge mir Mime,
sonst birgt er sich schwer meiner Geißel
Schwunge! Daß ich überall weile, wo keiner
mich wähnt, das weiß er, dünkt mich,
genau! Zögert ihr noch? Zaudert wohl gar?

Alberich:
Hither! Thither! Hehe! Hoho!
Lazy herd! Heap that pile on the Hoard!
There are heaps of Gold to pile on!
Get up, lazy one!
Despicable dogs! Put down the treasure!
Shall I help you? Bring it here!
(seeing Loge and Wotan)
Hey! Who is that over there?
Who has stolen in here?
Mime, you shabby scamp, come here!
Have you been chattering with these tramps?
Be off, you sluggard!
Get back to smelting and smithing!

Get to work! All of you, out of here!
Get below quickly!
Find me Gold from new veins!
Dig deep, or else my whip awaits you!

Mime will be watching that no one is idle!
I am everywhere, but no one can tell,
and no one can escape my whip!
Are you still lingering?
Are you still loitering?

He draws his ring from his finger, kisses it, and stretches it out threateningly.

Zitt're und zage, gezähmtes Heer!
Rasch gehorcht des Ringes Herrn!
Was wollt ihr hier?

Tremble in terror, and immediately obey the
great lord of the Ring!
What do you want here?

The Nibelungs, and Mime, howl and shriek as they disappear into clefts.
Alberich stares long and suspiciously at Wotan and Loge.

Wotan:
Von Nibelheims nächt'gem Land
vernahmen wir neue Mär':
mächt'ge Wunder wirke hier Alberich;
daran uns zu weiden trieb uns Gäste die Gier.

Alberich:
Nach Nibelheim führt euch der Neid:
so kühne Gäste, glaubt, kenn' ich gut!

Loge:
Kennst du mich gut, kindischer Alp?
Nun sag, wer bin ich daß du so bell'st?
Im kalten Loch, da kauernd du lag'st,
wer gab dir Licht und wärmende Lohe,
wenn Loge nie dir gelacht?
Was hülf dir dein Schmieden,
heizt' ich die Schmiede dir nicht?
Dir bin ich Vetter, und war dir Freund:
nicht fein drum dünkt mich dein Dank!

Alberich:
Den Lichtalben lacht jetzt Loge, der list'ge
Schelm?
Bist du Falscher ihr Freund,
wie mir Freund du einst war'st:
haha! mich freut's!
von ihnen fürcht' ich dann nichts.

Loge:
So denk' ich kannst du mir trau'n?

Alberich:
Deiner Untreu trau' ich,
nicht deiner Treu'!
Doch getrost trotz' ich euch Allen!

Loge:
Hohen Muth verleiht deine Macht;
grimmig groß wuchs dir die Kraft!

Alberich:
Siehst du den Hort,
den mein Heer dort mir gehäuft?

Loge:
So neidlichen sah ich noch nie.

Wotan:
We have heard rumors of Nibelheim's land
of night, and Alberich's wondrous marvels:
greed drove us here as guests so we could
gorge on them.

Alberich:
I well know such gallant guests: envy has
led you to Nibelheim!

Loge:
Do you really now me, childish imp?
Since you bark so much, then tell me who I am?
Loge provided comforting fire when you
were crouching in chilly caves without light
or heat?
Without my fires, you could not forge?
You're not being very friendly
or thankful to me:
I am your kinsman!

Alberich:
Loge, that cunning rogue,
now rejoices with the elves of light.
Are you now their friend, false one,
as you once were my friend?
I rejoice since I longer have anything to fear
from them!

Loge:
I thinks you can have faith in me?

Alberich:
I have faith in your faithlessness,
not in your fidelity!
I am undaunted and now defy all of you!

Loge:
Your power, and your great might and
strength now gives you assurance!

Alberich:
Do you see the Hoard that my henchmen
have piled up for me?

Loge:
I never saw such envy.

Alberich:
Das ist für heut', ein kärglich Häufchen!
Kühn und mächtig soll er künftig sich mehren.

Alberich:
That is just today's scanty pile!
It will increase dramatically hereafter.

Wotan:
Zu was doch frommt dir der Hort,
da freudlos Nibelheim,
und nichts für Schätze hier feil?

Wotan:
But what value is the Hoard, since
Nibelheim is joyless, and the treasures can
buy nothing here?

Alberich:
Schätze zu schaffen, und Schätze zu bergen
nützt mir Nibelheims Nacht.
Doch mit dem Hort, in der Höhle gehäuft,
denk' ich dann Wunder zu wirken: die ganze
Welt gewinn' ich mit ihm mir zu eigen!

Alberich:
Nibelheim's night serves me to create and
conceal treasure,
but with the Hoard piled here in the cave,
I intend to work wonders with it:
I will win the entire world for myself!

Wotan:
Wie beginnst du, Gütiger, das?

Wotan:
How will you achieve that, good friend?

Alberich:
Die in linder Lüfte Weh'n da oben ihr lebt,
lacht und liebt: mit gold'ner Faust euch
Göttliche fang' ich mir alle!

Alberich:
You love and rejoice living aloft among the
soft zephyr breezes: I'll capture all of the
Gods, and seize them in my grasp!

Wie ich der Liebe abgesagt,
Alles was lebt soll ihr entsagen!
Mit Golde gekirrt, nach Gold,
nur sollt ihr noch gieren!
Auf wonnigen Höh'n, in seligem Weben
wiegt ihr euch; den Schwarzalben verachtet
ihr ewigen Schwelger!

As I foreswore love,
all living things shall renounce it!
You shall be enchanted
by the allure of Gold.
You now live on radiant heights,
lulled into bliss.
The dark elves despise you eternal revelers!

Habt Acht! Habt Acht!
Denn dient ihr Männer erst meiner Macht,
eure schmucken Frau'n,
die mein Frei'n verschmäht,
sie zwingt zur Lust sich der Zwerg,
lacht Liebe ihm nicht!

Beware! Beware!
For when you shall bow to my might,
then the Dwarf
will steal his pleasure with your pretty
women; they scorned his wooing,
although love does not smile upon him!

Ha ha ha ha!
Habt ihr's gehört? Habt Acht!
Habt Acht! vor dem nächtlichen Heer,
entsteigt des Niblungen Hort
aus stummer Tiefe zu Tag!

Ha ha ha ha!
Do you hear?
Beware the hosts of the night:
in the daylight, the Niblung Hoard
shall rise from the silent depths!

Wotan:
Vergeh', frevelnder Gauch!

Wotan: *(violently)*
Enough, impious fool!

Alberich:
Was sagt der?

Loge:
Sei doch bei Sinnen!
Wen doch faßte nicht Wunder,
erfährt er Alberichs Werk?

Gelingt deiner herrlichen List,
was mit dem Horte du heischest:
den Mächtigsten muß ich dich rühmen;
denn Mond und Stern', und die strahlende
Sonne, sie auch dürfen nicht anders,
dienen müssen sie dir.

Doch wichtig acht' ich vor allem,
daß des Hortes Häufer,
der Niblungen Heer neidlos dir geneigt.
Einen Reif rührtest du kühn;
dem zagte zitternd dein Volk:
doch, wenn im Schlaf ein Dieb dich
beschlich,
den Ring schlau dir entriss',
wie wahrtest du, Weiser, dich dann?

Alberich:
Der listigste dünkt sich Loge;
andre denkt er immer sich dumm:
daß sein' ich bedürfte zu Rath und Dienst,
um harten Dank, das hörte der Dieb jetzt gern!

Den hehlenden Helm ersann ich mir selbst;
der sorglichste Schmied, Mime, mußt' ihn
mir schmieden: schnell mich zu wandeln,
nach meinem Wunsch die Gestalt
mir zu tauschen, taugt der Helm.

Niemand sieht mich, wenn er mich sucht;
doch überall bin ich, geborgen dem Blick.
So, ohne Sorge bin ich selbst sicher vor dir,
du fromm sorgender Freund!

Loge:
Vieles sah ich, Seltsames fand ich,
doch solches Wunder gewahrt' ich nie.

Alberich:
What did he say?

Loge: *(intervening, to Alberich)*
Let's not lose our senses!
Who would not be seized with wonder,
by Alberich's work?

I proclaim you the mightiest,
since your masterful cunning
with your treasure
can achieve anything you ask;
even the moon and stars and the sun
can not withstand your power.

But I deem it significant that those who
heap the Gold for the Niblung,
should serve him ungrudgingly.
You boldly fashioned a Ring
before which your people tremble
and cower in fear.
But, crafty one, how would you protect
yourself if a thief stealthily stole the Ring
from you while you slept?

Alberich:
Loge considers himself the most cunning.
He believes that I need his wisdom and
counsel to thwart a thief!
I myself conceived the magic Tarnhelm.

Mime, the most skilful smith forged it for
me.
The helmet allows me
to transform myself at will,
and swiftly change my shape.

No one can see me athough they search.
I am everywhere, but hidden from sight.
In that way, I can live carefree, even
from you, my kind and thoughtful friend!

Loge:
I have seen many wonders but never
witnessed such a marvel.

Dem Werk ohne Gleichen
kann ich nicht glauben;
wäre das eine möglich,
deine Macht währte dann ewig!

This work is without equal
and no one would believe it;
but with this possibility,
your power would be unending!

Alberich:
Mein'st du, ich lüg' und prahle wie Loge?

Alberich:
Do you think I lie and boast like Loge?

Loge:
Bis ich's geprüft, bezweifl' ich, Zwerg, dein Wort.

Loge:
I doubt your word, Dwarf, until I see it for myself.

Alberich:
Vor Klugheit bläht sich zum platzen der Blöde! Nun plage dich Neid!
Bestimm', in welcher Gestalt soll ich jach vor dir steh'n?

Alberich:
The fool's vanity is bursting!
Now let envy devour you!
Command a shape in which I can suddenly appear before you!

Loge:
In welcher du willst;
nur mach' vor Staunen mich stumm!

Loge:
Change into whatever shape you wish:
make me dumb with amazement!

Alberich:
"Riesenwurm winde sich ringelnd!"

Alberich: *(puts the Tarnhelm on his head)*
"Giant snake, wind and coil thee!"

***Alberich immediately disappears. In his place a huge serpent writhes on the floor;
it lifts its head and stretches its open jaws toward Wotan and Loge.***

Loge:
Ohe! Ohe!
Schreckliche Schlange, verschlinge mich nicht! Schone Logen das Leben!

Loge: *(pretends to be seized with terror)*
Ohe! Ohe!
Terrible Dragon, do not swallow me!
Spare Loge's life!

Wotan:
Ha ha ha! Ha ha ha!
Gut, Alberich! Gut, du Arger!
Wie wuchs so rasch zum riesigen Wurme der Zwerg!

Wotan:
Ha ha ha! Ha ha ha!
Good, Alberich! Good, You rascal!
How quickly the Dwarf turned into a monstrous Dragon!

The dragon disappears and immediately after, Alberich is seen in its place.

Alberich:
Hehe! Ihr Klugen! glaubt ihr mir nun?

Alberich:
Do you believe me now, clever ones?

Loge:
Mein Zittern mag dir's bezeugen!
Zur großen Schlange schuf'st du dich schnell: weil ich's gewahrt, willig glaub' ich dem Wunder.

Loge: *(in a trembling voice)*
My trembling proves it!
You swiftly made yourself into a giant snake! I have seen it!
It's a marvel!

Doch, wie du wuchsest, kannst du auch
winzig und klein dich schaffen?

But, you grew larger; can you make
yourself smaller?

Das Klügste schien' mir das,
Gefahren schlau zu entfliehn:
das aber dünkt mich zu schwer!

That seems to me the shrewdest way to
escape danger, but I think that would
be too difficult!

Alberich:
Zu schwer dir, weil du zu dumm!
Wie klein soll ich sein?

Alberich:
Too hard for you because you're stupid!
How small shall I be?

Loge:
Daß die feinste Klinze dich fasse,
wo bang die Kröte sich birgt.

Loge:
Where the narrowest cranny could hold
you; where a frightened toad might hide.

Alberich:
Pah! Nichts leichter! Luge du her!
"Krumm und grau krieche Kröte!"

Alberich: *(putting on the Tarnhelm)*
Pah! Nothing is simpler! Look at me now!
"Crawl over here, crooked toad!"

Alberich disappears. A toad crawls toward them.

Loge:
Dort, die Kröte! Greife sie rasch!

Loge: *(to Wotan)*
There's the toad, capture it quickly!

Wotan places his foot on the toad. Loge grabs its head.
Alberich becomes suddenly visible in his own form, writhing under Wotan's foot.

Alberich:
Ohe! Verflucht! Ich bin gefangen!

Alberich:
Curse you! You've captured me!

Loge:
Hal" ihn fest, bis ich ihn band.
Nun schnell hinauf: dort ist er unter!

Loge:
Hold him fast until I tie him up.
Let's quickly go up: he is ours!

Loge binds Alberich's hands and feet; he struggles violently.
They drag him into the shaft and disappear with him.

Wotan and Loge, with Alberich bound, emerge from the cleft.

END of SCENE 3

Scene 4

An open space on a mountaintop; it is shrouded in a pale mist.

Loge:
Da, Vetter, sitze du fest!
Luge, Liebster, dort liegt die Welt,
die du Lungrer gewinnen dir willst: welch
Stellchen, sag', bestimmst du drin mir zum Stall?

Loge:
Sit down, my friend.
Look around, there lies the world,
that you yearned to win.
What place do you assign there for me?

Alberich:
Schändlicher Schächer!
Du Schalk! Du Schelm!
Löse den Bast, binde mich los;
den Frevel sonst büßest du Frecher!

Alberich:
Infamous scoundrel!
You rogue!
Loosen the rope, and let me go free;
don't bind my arms or you'll regret it!

Wotan:
Gefangen bist du, fest mir gefesselt,
wie du die Welt, was lebt und webt,
in deiner Gewalt schon wähntest,
in Banden liegst du vor mir,
du Banger kannst es nicht läugnen!
Zu ledigen dich, bedarf's nun der Lösung.

Wotan:
You are my captive now.
You did believe you had won the world,
but now you are bound at my feet.
Don't deny it, you're immobile.
But before we release you
we want the ransom!

Alberich:
O ich Tropf! Ich träumender Thor!
wie dumm traut' ich dem diebischen Trug!
furchtbare Rache räche den Fehl!

Alberich:
What folly! I blindly trusted the
treacherous thief! I'll vent my anger with a
terrible revenge!

Loge:
Soll Rache dir frommen, vor Allem rathe
dich frei: dem gebund'nen Manne büßt kein
Freier den Frevel.
Drum sinn'st du auf Rache,
rasch ohne Säumen
sorg' um die Lösung zunächst!

Loge:
Are you thirsting for revenge?
First free youself;
you must be free
to fulfill your revenge.
As you dream of vengeance,
don't forget our ransom demand!

Alberich:
So heischt was ihr begehrt!

Alberich: *(harshly)*
Then tell me what I must give you!

Wotan:
Den Hort und dein helles Gold.

Wotan:
The Hoard and your sparkling Gold.

Alberich:
Gieriges Gaunergezücht!
(Doch behalt' ich mir nur den Ring, des
Hortes entrath' ich dann leicht; denn von
Neuem gewonnen und wonnig genährt!)

Alberich:
Gluttonous thieves!
(If only I could only keep the Ring
for myself,
and leave them the Hoard!)

Ist er bald durch des Ringes Gebot:
eine Witzigung wär's, die weise mich macht;
zu theuer nicht zahl' ich die Zucht,
lass' für die Lehre ich den Tand.

And remind myself
that I still know how to fashion the Ring;
its loss is not so dear
if that is all I lose.

Wotan:
Erleg'st du den Hort?

Wotan:
Do you yield the Hoard to us?

Alberich:
Löst mir die Hand, so ruf' ich ihn her.

Alberich:
Untie my hand and I'll summon it.

Loge unties the rope from Alberich's right hand.
Alberich touches the Ring with his lips and murmurs a secret command.

Wohlan, die Niblungen rief ich mir nah'.
Ihrem Herrn gehorchend, hör' ich den Hort
aus der Tiefe sie führen zu Tag!

Behold, the Nibelungs are called by their
master. Watch how they hawl the Hoard
into the daylight!

Nun löst mich vom lästigen Band!

Loosen those torturous cords!

Wotan:
Nicht eh'r, bis alles gezahlt!

Wotan:
Not until we have been paid!

The Nibelungs pile up the hoard.

Alberich:
O schändliche Schmach!
daß die scheuen Knechte geknebelt selbst
mich erschau'n!

Alberich:
What shame and disgrace, that my shrinking
vassals should see me shackled!
There, let it sit there in a pile!

Dorthin geführt, wie ichos befehl'!
All zu Hauf schichtet den Hort!
Helf' ich euch Lahmen? Hieher nicht gelugt!
Rasch da! rasch!
Dann rührt euch von hinnen,
daß ihr mir schafft! Fort in die Schachte!
Weh' euch, treff' ich euch faul!
Auf den Fersen folg' ich euch nach!

Dolts! Don't look at me!
Let it rest in a pile!
Over there, quickly!
Off to your tasks,
and your smithing!
Back to the tunnels!
If there are idlers,
If need be, Ill be at your back in an instant!

Alberich kisses his Ring and stretches it out commandingly. As if struck by a blow,
the Nibelungs become terrified, rush into the cleft, and quickly disappear.

Gezahlt hab' ich; nun lass' mich zieh'n:
und das Helmgeschmeid', das Loge dort
hält, das gebt mir nun gütlich zurück!

There lies your ransom; now let me go.
And the Tarnhelm that Loge is holdings,
kindly give it back to me!

Loge:
Zur Buße gehört auch die Beute.

Loge: *(throwing the Tarnhelm on the Hoard)*
This is part of the plunder.

Alberich:
Verfluchter Dieb! Doch, nur Geduld!
Der den alten mir schuf, schafft einen
andern: noch halt' ich die Macht, der Mime
gehorcht.

Alberich:
Accursed thief! But wait a while!
Mime still obeys my power
and if I should command it,
he'll make another Ring.

Schlimm zwar ist's, dem schlauen Feind
zu lassen die listige Wehr!
Nun denn! Alberich ließ euch Alles:
jetzt lös't, ihr Bösen, das Band!

It is sad that my hated foes
should take advantage of my weak defenses!
Well, Alberich has given you everything,
so now loosen these bonds!

Loge:
Bist du befriedigt? Lass' ich ihn frei?

Loge: *(to Wotan)*
Are you content now? Shall I free him?

Wotan:
Ein gold'ner Ring ragt dir am Finger:
hörst du, Alp?
der, acht' ich, gehört mit zum Hort.

Wotan: *(to Alberich)*
A golden Ring gleams on your finger:
Dwarf, do you hear me?
That Ring also belongs with the Hoard.

Alberich:
Der Ring?

Alberich: *(horrified)*
The Ring?

Wotan:
Zu deiner Lösung mußt du ihn lassen.

Wotan:
That must also be ours, before we free you.

Alberich:
Das Leben, doch nicht den Ring!

Alberich: *(trembling)*
Take my life, but not the Ring!

Wotan:
Den Reif verlang' ich mit dem Leben mach',
was du willst.

Wotan: *(more violently)*
Surrender the Ring, or your life!

Alberich:
Lös' ich mir Leib' und Leben,
den Ring auch muß ich mir lösen.

Hand und Haupt, Aug' und Ohr sind nicht
mehr mein Eigen, als hier dieser rote Ring!

Alberich:
If life and limbs are left to me, then the Ring
must also be mine!

Hand and head, and eyes and ears are not as
important to me as possessomg this Ring!

Wotan:
Dein Eigen nennst du den Ring?
Rasest du, schamloser Albe?
Nüchtern sag', wem entnahmst du das
Gold, daraus du den schimmernden schuf'st?

Wotan:
You say the Ring belongs to you?
You raving, impudent imp?
Be honest, tell me how you got the Gold
from which you fashioned the Ring?

War's dein Eigen, was du Arger der
Wassertiefe entwandt?
Bei des Rheines Töchtern hole dir Rath,
ob ihr Gold sie zu eigen dir gaben, das du
zum Ring dir geraubt!

Did the Gold sitting in the Rhine depths
belong to you?
Are you implying that the river maidens are
lying, and that they stole the Gold from
you?

Alberich:
Schmähliche Tücke! Schändlicher Trug!
Wirfst du Schächer die Schuld mir vor,
die dir so wonnig erwünscht?

Alberich:
Infamous tricksters! What shameful deceit!
Thief, you blame me for stealing something
that you were obsessed to possess?

Wie gern raubtest du selbst
dem Rheine das Gold, war nur so leicht die
Kunst, es zu schmieden, erlangt?

How gladly you would have robbed the
Rhine's Gold yourself, if you had found a
way to forge the Gold!

Wie glückt' es nun dir Gleißner zum Heil,
daß der Niblung, ich, aus schmählicher
Noth, in des Zornes Zwange,
den schrecklichen Zauber gewann,
dess Werk nun lustig dir lacht?

You hypocrite, how well it ultimately
turned out that I, the Nibelung, in shame
and distress, and maddened by fury, gained
the terrible magic
whose work now possesses you.

Des Unseligen, Angst versehrten
fluchfertige, furchtbare That,
zu fürstlichem Tand soll sie fröhlich dir
taugen, zur Freude dir frommen mein Fluch?
Hüte dich, herrischer Gott!

Must this fearful deed,
from one wretched and wracked with fear,
serve you as a royal toy: serve you for your
pleasure?
Take heed, haughty God!

Frevelte ich, so frevelt' ich frei an mir:
doch an Allem was war, ist und wird,
frevelst, Ewiger, du,
entreißest du frech mir den Ring!

If I sinned I did so against myself,
but you immoral one, if you rashly seize
my Ring, you will have sinned against all
that was, all that is, and all that shall be!

Wotan:
Her der Ring! Kein Recht an ihm
schwörst du schwatzend dir zu.

Wotan:
Yield the Ring! Your babbling proves that
you have no right to it.

Wotan seizes Alberich, and violently pulls the Ring from his finger.

Alberich:
Zertrümmert! Zerknickt!
Der Traurigen traurigster Knecht!

Alberich: *(shrieking horribly)*
Defeated! Destroyed!
A vassal of the most wretched slave!

Wotan:
Nun halt' ich, was mich erhebt,
der Mächtigen mächtigsten Herrn.

Wotan: *(contemplating the Ring)*
Now I possess what will make me the
mightiest of all the God.

Wotan places the Ring on his finger.

Loge:
Ist er gelöst?

Wotan:
Bind' ihn los!

Loge:
Schlüpfe denn heim!
Keine Schlinge hält dich:
frei fahre dahin!

Alberich:
Bin ich nun frei? Wirklich frei?

So grüß' euch denn meiner Freiheit
erster Gruß!
Wie durch Fluch er mir gerieth,
verflucht sei dieser Ring!
Gab sein Gold mir Macht ohne Maaß,
nun zeug' sein Zauber Tod dem, der ihn trägt!
Kein Froher soll seiner sich freu'n,
keinem Glücklichen lache sein lichter Glanz!

Wer ihn besitzt, den sehre die Sorge,
und wer ihn nicht hat den nage der Neid!
Jeder giere nach seinem Gut,
doch keiner genieße mit Nutzen sein!
Ohne Wucher hüt' ihn sein Herr;
doch den Würger zieh' er ihm zu!
Dem Tode verfallen feßle den Feigen die
Furcht: so lang' er lebt sterb' er lechzend
dahin, des Ringes Herr als des Ringes Knecht!

Bis in meiner Hand
den geraubten wieder ich halte!

So segnet in höchster Noth der Nibelung
seinen Ring: behalt' ihn nun, hüte ihn wohl!
Meinem Fluch fliehest du nicht.

Loge: *(to Wotan)*
Shall he go free?

Wotan:
Set him free!

Loge: *(to Alberich, after releasing him)*
Slip away to your home!
Go free from here, there are no more
shackles to bond you!

Alberich: *(raising himself)*
Am I now free? Really free?

Then listen to my freedom's first greeting!
Since it came to be by a Curse,
accursed this Ring shall be!
Since its Gold
gave me measureless might!
death shall seize whoever wears it!
It shall no longer gladden anyone with its
luster; it shall gnaw its holder with envy!

Each shall tremble to possess it,
but none shall find pleasure with it!
Its owner
shall reap no gain,
because through it
he meets his executioner!
The fear of death
becomes his fancy,
and he shall languish as he yearns to die!

The master of the Ring shall be its slave,
until I again possess what was stolen!

Now I bless the Nibelung's Ring.
I give it you with care, but you cannot flee
from my Curse!

Alberich vanishes quickly into a crevice. The dense mist gradually clears.

Loge:
Lauschtest du seinem Liebesgruß?

Wotan:
Gönn' ihm die geifernde Lust!

Loge:
Heed love's farewell?

Wotan: *(contemplating the Ring)*
Let him give vent to his fury!

Loge:
Fasolt und Fafner nahen von fern:
Freia führen sie her.

Loge: *(looking to the right)*
Fasolt and Fafner are approaching.
They're bringing Freia back!

Donner, Froh and Fricka appear through the gradually dispersing mist.

Froh:
Sie kehrten zurück!

Froh:
They have returned!

Donner:
Willkommen, Bruder!

Donner:
Welcome, brother!

Fricka:
Bringst du gute Kunde?

Fricka: *(anxiously to Wotan)*
Do you bring good news?

Loge:
Mit List und Gewalt gelang das Werk:
dort liegt, was Freia lös't.

Loge: *(pointing to the Hoard)*
We completed the task by cunning and force
task: there is Freia's ransom.

Donner:
Aus der Riesen Haft naht dort die Holde.

Donner:
One of the Giant's is holding her.

Froh:
Wie liebliche Luft wieder uns weht,
wonnig Gefühl die Sinne erfüllt!
Traurig ging' es uns allen,
getrennt für immer von ihr,
die leidlos ewiger Jugend
jubelnde Lust uns verleiht.

Froh:
The balm of those wondrous soft breezes
fill our senses again!
It would be dark and gloomy if we are ever
separated from her again; she provides us
with pain-free, eternal youth: a rapturous
joyous delight!

Brightness returns. The Gods have regained their former pristine freshness.
A misty veil hovers so that the distant fortress remains invisible.
Fasolt and Fafner enter, leading Freia between them.
Fricka hastens joyfully toward her sister, and embraces her.

Fricka:
Lieblichste Schwester, süßeste Lust!
bist du mir wieder gewonnen?

Fricka:
Dear sister, our dearest delight:
you have once again joined us?

Fasolt:
Halt! Nicht sie berührt! Noch gehört sie
uns.
Auf Riesenheims ragender Mark rasteten
wir; mit treuem Muth des Vertrages Pfand
pflegten wir.
So sehr mich's reut, zurück doch bring'
ich's, erlegt uns Brüdern die Lösung ihr.

Fricka: *(restraining her)*
Hold on! Don't touch her yet! She still
belongs to us!
We stopped to rest at Reisenheim.
We are keeping our pledge to honor the
treaty with you.
I've brought her here so you can now pay
us the ransom.

Wotan:
Bereit liegt die Lösung:
des Goldes Maaß sei nun gütlich gemessen.

Wotan:
The ransom is ready for you; the mount of
Gold shall be fully measured.

Fasolt:
Das Weib zu missen,
wisse, gemuthet mich weh': soll aus dem
Sinn sie mir schwinden, des Geschmeides
Hort häufet denn so, daß meinem Blick die
Blühende ganz er verdeck'!

Fasolt:
My spirits are so sad to have to lose this
woman; if she is to be truly erased from my
mind, the Hoard must be heaped so high
that it completely hides the lovely woman
from my sight!

Wotan:
So stellt das Maaß nach Freias Gestalt!

Wotan:
Freia's form shall become the measure!

*The two Giants place Freia bettween them. They place their poles into the ground in front
of Freia, so that she becomes the guide to measure the height and breadth of the Hoard.*

Fafner:
Gepflanzt sind die Pfähle nach Pfandes
Maaß; gehäuft nun füll es den Hort!

Fafner:
The poles we've planted will frame her
form; we'll heap the Hoard to he height!

Wotan:
Eilt mit dem Werk: widerlich ist mir's!

Wotan:
Hurry up with this work: it sorely irks me!

Loge:
Hilf mir, Froh!

Loge:
Help me, Froh!

Froh:
Freias Schmach eil' ich zu enden.

Froh:
I'll hurry to end your shame.

Loge and Froh hastily pile up the treasure between the poles.

Fafner:
Nicht so leicht und locker gefügt.

Fafner:
Don't pile the Gold so loosely.

Fafner tamps the treasure firmly.
He finds some crevices and orders them to be filled tightly.

Fest und dicht füll 'er das Mass! Hier lug'
ich noch durch: verstopft mir die Lücken!

Fill it firm and tight!
I can still see though some of these holes!

Loge:
Zurück, du Grober!

Loge:
Stand back, clod, and keep your hands off!

Fafner:
Hierher! Die Klinze verklemmt!

Fafner:
Here, close these crevices!

Wotan:
Tief in der Brust brennt mir die Schmach!

Wotan: *(turning away, annoyed)*
Disgrace burns deep in my heart!

Fricka:
Sieh, wie in Scham
schmählich die Edle steht:
um Erlösung fleht stumm der leidende Blick.
Böser Mann!
der Minnigen botest du das!

Fricka: *(staring at Freia)*
See how our treasured Goddess stands
there, shamed and humiliated:
her anguished look yearns for her release.
Heartless man! How do you ask this of a
loved one!

Fafner:
Noch mehr! Noch mehr hierher!

Fafner:
Still more! There's still more to pile on!

Donner:
Kaum halt' ich mich; schäumende Wuth
weckt mir der schamlose Wicht!
Hierher, du Hund! Willst du messen,
so miß' dich selber mit mir!

Donner:
I can scarcely contain myself from this
rogue!
Come here, you hound, if you want to
measure, do it against me!

Fafner:
Ruhig, Donner! Rolle, wo's taugt:
hier nützt dein Rasseln dir nichts.

Fafner:
Calm down, Donner, your thunder does not
serve you here.

Donner:
Nicht dich Schmähl'chen zu zerschmettern?

Donner: *(threatening)*
It will serve to crush a scoundre!

Wotan:
Friede doch!
Schon dünkt mich Freia verdeckt.

Wotan:
Let's have peace, my friend!
I think Freia is completely covered now.

Fafner measures the Hoard, and meticulosly looks for crevices.

Loge:
Der Hort ging auf.

Loge:
The Hoard is finished!.

Fafner:
Noch schimmert mir Holdas Haar:
Dort das Gewirk wirf auf den Hort!

Fafner:
I can see Holda's hair shining.
Throw that other thing on the Hoard!

Loge:
Wie? Auch den Helm?

Loge:
What? The hemlet too?

Fafner:
Hurtig, her mit ihm!

Fafner:
Quickly, get over here with it!

Wotan:
Lass' ihn denn fahren!

Wotan:
Let that go also!

Loge throws the Tarnhelm on the Hoard.

Loge:
So sind wir denn fertig! Seid ihr zufrieden?

Loge:
We're finished! Are you content now?

Fasolt:
Freia, die Schöne, schau' ich nicht mehr:
so ist sie gelös't? muß ich sie lassen?

Fasolt:
Freia, fair one, I see her no more:
is she then released? Must I let her go?

He goes up close and peers through the Hoard.

Weh! Noch blitzt ihr Blick zu mir her;
des Auges Stern strahlt mich noch an;
durch eine Spalte muß ich's erspäh'n.
Seh' ich diess wonnige Auge,
von dem Weibe lass ich nicht ab!

Her gaze still excites me!
Her eyes shine through the cracks like
beaming stars.
As long as I can see those lovely eyes,
I cannot tear myself away from her!

Fafner:
He! Euch rath' ich, verstopft mir die Ritze!

Fafner:
Hey! I advise you to fill in this crevice!

Loge:
Nimmersatte! seht ihr denn nicht,
ganz schwand uns der Hort?

Loge:
Insatiable! Can't you see that all the Gold is
piled on the Hoard?

Fafner:
Mit nichten, Freund! an Wotans Finger
glänzt von Gold noch ein Ring:
den gebt, die Ritze zu füllen!

Fafner:
Not so, friend! The Golden Ring still shines
on Wotan's finger. Give it to me to fill in the
opening!

Wotan:
Wie? Diesen Ring?

Wotan:
What? This my Ring?

Loge:
Laßt euch rathen! Den Rheintöchtern gehört
dies Gold; ihnen gibt Wotan es wieder.

Loge:
Listen! The Gold still belongs to the Rhine
maidens. Wotan will give it back to them!

Wotan:
Was schwatzest du da?
Was schwer ich mir erbeutet,
ohne Bangen wahr' ich's für mich!

Wotan:
What's all that prattling about?
I won the prize without guilt,
so I'm going to keep it for myself!

Loge:
Schlimm dann steht's um mein Versprechen,
das ich den Klagenden gab!

Loge:
Then the promise I gave the Rhinemaidens
has been broken.

Wotan:
Dein Versprechen bindet mich nicht:
als Beute bleibt mir der Reif.

Wotan:
Your contract does not bind me; the Ring
remains with me as booty.

Fafner:
Doch hier zur Lösung mußt du ihn legen.

Fafner:
Yield it to us as part of the ransom.

Wotan:
Fordert frech was ihr wollt,
alles gewähr' ich; um alle Welt
doch nicht fahren lass' ich den Ring!

Wotan:
You can boldly make your demands,
but nothing in the world will make me
surrender the Ring.

Fasolt:
Aus dann ist's, beim Alten bleibt's;
nun folgt uns Freia für immer!

Fasalt: *(pulls Freia from behind the Hoard)*
Then it's finished. Freia will follow us
according to our original agreement!

Freia:
Hülfe! Hülfe!

Freia:
Help me! Help me!

Fricka:
Harter Gott! gib ihnen nach!

Fricka:
Cruel god! Give them what they want!

Froh:
Spare das Gold nicht!

Froh:
Don't hold back the Gold!

Donner:
Spende den Ring doch!

Donner:
Give them the Ring!

Fafner restrains Fasolt, who is agitating to leave.

Wotan:
Lasst mich in Ruh! Den Reif geb'ich nicht!

Wotan:
Leave me in peace: the Ring is mine!

Wotan turns away from them in anger. A bluish light appears from a rocky cleft.
Erda suddenly becomes visible, rising from below to half her height.

Erda:
Weiche, Wotan! Weiche!
Flieh' des Ringes Fluch!
Rettungslos dunk'lem Verderben
weih't dich sein Gewinn.

Erda: *(warningly toward Wotan)*
Yield it, Wotan! Yield it!
Escape from the Ring's deadly curse!
You'll be doomed to destruction if you
don't return it.

Wotan:
Wer bist du mahnendes Weib?

Wotan:
Who's threatening me?

Erda:
Wie alles war weiß ich;
wie alles wird, wie alles sein wird:
seh' ich auch der ew'gen Welt Urwala, Erda,
mahnt deinen Muth.

Erda:
I know whatever is; whatever was; and
whatever will be.
It is I, Erda, who calls you:
the ancestress of the eternal world.

Drei der Töchter,
ur-erschaff'ne, gebar mein Schoß; was ich
sehe, sagen dir nächtlich die Nornen.
Doch höchste Gefahr führt mich heut'
selbst zu dir her.
Höre! Höre! Höre!
Alles was ist, endet!
Ein düstrer Tag dämmert den Göttern:
dir rath' ich, meide den Ring!

I bore three daughters,
who were conceived before time began.
What I see, the Norns tell you nightly.
But today, the greatest danger
brings me to you in person.
Hear me! Hear me! Hear me!
All that is, shall conme to an end!
A dark day dawns for the Gods:
be wise and give up the Ring!

As Erda sinks slowly into the earth; the bluish light begins to fade.

Wotan:
Geheimniss hehr hallt mir dein Wort:
weile, daß mehr ich wisse!

Wotan:
Your words are mysteriously striking:
stay here so that I may learn more!

Erda:
Ich warnte dich; du weißt genug:
sinn' in Sorg' und Furcht!

Erda: *(disappearing)*
I warned you; you know enough to reflect
on the imminent dangers!

Wotan:
Soll ich sorgen und fürchten,
dich muß ich fassen, alles erfahren!

Wotan:
I've become tormented; I must seize you
and learn everything!

Froh and Fricka restrain Wotan.

Fricka:
Was willst du, Wüthender?

Fricka:
What now, mad man?

Froh:
Halt' ein, Wotan!
Scheue die Edle, achte ihr Wort!

Froh:
Don't go! Wotan! Don't touch the noble
soul, but heed her well!

Donner:
Hört, ihr Riesen! Zurück, und harret!
das Gold wird euch gegeben.

Donner: *(turns with resolve to the Giants)*
Hey, Giants, come back and collect your
ransom.

Freia:
Darf ich es hoffen?
Dünkt euch Holda wirklich der Lösung
werth?

Freia:
Dare I hope so?
Do you think Holda is truly worth such a
ransom?

Wotan:
Zu mir, Freia! Du bist befreit.
Wieder gekauft
kehr' uns die Jugend zurück!
Ihr Riesen, nehmt euren Ring!

Wotan:
Come to me, Freia, and be free!
You Giants, come and take the Ring,
so that now we shall once again
have our youth restored!

Wotan throws the Ring onto the Hoard. The Giants release Freia.
Fafner spreads out a huge sack in preparaion of packing the Hoard.

Fasolt:
Halt, du Gieriger!
Gönne mir auch was!
Redliche Theilung taugt uns beiden.

Fasolt: *(to Fafner)*
Stop, greedy one!
Leave some for me too!
A fair split would be best for both of us!

Fafner:
Mehr an der Maid als am Gold
lag dir verliebtem Geck:
mit Müh zum Tausch vermocht' ich dich
Thoren;
ohne zu theilen, hättest du Freia gefreit:
theil ich den Hort,
billig behalt' ich die größte Hälfte für mich!

Fafner:
You long more for the maid than the Gold,
lovesick one! It was difficult for me to
persuade you to exchange her for the Gold.
If you won Freia you wouldn't have shared
her, so I'm dividing up the treasure
and rightly retaining the larger part
for myself.

Fasolt:
Schändlicher du! Mir diesen Schimpf?

Euch ruf ich zu Richtern:
theilet nach Recht uns redlich den Hort!

Fasolt:
You swindler! Are you vilifying me?

Gods, I call on you as judges to fairly divide
the treasure between us!

Loge:
Den Hort lass' ihn raffen;
halte du nur auf den Ring!

Loge: *(to Fasolt)*
Let them take the treasure;
just keep the Ring for youself!

Fasolt:
Zurück! Du Frecher! Mein ist der Ring;
mir blieb er für Freias Blick!

Fasolt: *(throws himself on Fafner)*
Get back! The Ring is mine, because it
prompted Freia's gaze on me!

Fafner:
Fort mit der Faust! Der Ring ist mein!

Fafner: *(snatches the Ring from him)*
Don't touch it! The Ring is mine!

Fasolt:
Ich halt' ihn, mir gehört er!

Fasolt: *(seizes the Ring from Fafner)*
I have it, it belongs to me!

Fafner:
Halt' ihn fest, daß er nicht fall'!

Fafner: *(strikes Fasolt with his staff)*
Hold it fast in case it should fall!

Fasolt falls after one blow: Fafner then wrests the Ring from his brother.

Nun blinzle nach Freias Blick!
An den Reif rühr'st du nicht mehr!

Now look upon Freia's piercing gaze!
You will no longer see the Ring!

Fafner places the Ring into the sack and quietly proceeds to pack the Hoard.
The Gods stand horrified. There is a long and solemn silence.

Wotan:
Furchtbar nun erfind' ich des Fluches Kraft!

Wotan: *(deeply moved)*
I fear the curse's power!

Loge:
Was gleicht, Wotan, wohl deinem Glücke?
Viel erwarb dir des Ringes Gewinn;
daß er nun dir genommen, nützt dir noch
mehr: deine Feinde—sieh!—fällen sich
selbst um das Gold, das du vergab'st.

Loge:
Wotan, nothing equals your luck.
You agonized when you won the Ring,
but it is better that it was returnend;
your foes committed murder for the old
trinket that you gave up!

Wotan:
Wie doch Bangen mich bindet!
Sorg und Furcht fesseln den Sinn:
wie sie zu enden, lehre mich Erda:
zu ihr muß ich hinab!

Wotan:
A dark foreboding overcomes me!
Fear and anxiety occupy my mind.
How can I end it?
I must find Erda; she will teach me!

Fricka:
Wo weil'st du, Wotan?
Winkt dir nicht hold die hehre Burg,
die des Gebieters gastlich bergend nun harrt?

Fricka: *(caressing him cajolingly)*
Why do you remain here, Wotan?
Doesn't our proud fortress beckon you?
It waits to welcome and shelter its lord.

Wotan:
Mit bösem Zoll zahl't ich den Bau.

Wotan: *(gloomily)*
I paid for this work with tarnished wages!

Donner:
Schwüles Gedünst schwebt in der Luft;
lästig ist mir der trübe Druck!
Das bleiche Gewölk samml' ich zu
blitzendem Wetter,
das fegt den Himmel mir hell.

Donner: *(pointing to Valhalla)*
Sultry mists hang in the air;
its heavy weight oppresses me!
I'll collect the hovering lightning and
thunder clouds,
and clear the sky!

Donner mounts a high rock, and swings his hammer as mists collect around him.

Zu mir, du Gedüft! Ihr Dünste zu mir!
Donner, der Herr, ruft euch zu Heer!

Heda! Heda! Hedo!
Miss, come to me! Vapors, come!

Aud des Hammers Schwung
schwebet herbei:
He da! He da!
duftig Gedünst'
Donner ruft euchzu Heer!
Heda! Heda! Hedo!

Lord Donner summons you to his master!
Let my hammer swing and sweep away
the fog and wandering mists! He da! He da!
Vapors, come to me!
Donner, your master, summons your host!
Heda! Heda! Hedo!

Donner vanishes behind a thickening thundercloud.
At the stroke of his hammer, a vivid flash of lightning comes from the cloud;
a shatttering thunderclap follows. Froh has disappeared into the clouds.

Bruder, hieher!
Weise der Brücke den Weg!

Brother, come here!
Show them the path over the bridge!

Suddenly the clouds disperse; Donner and Froh become visible:
from their feet a rainbow bridge stretches with blinding radiance across the valley
to the fortress, that now glows in the light of the setting sun.

Fafner collects the entire Hoard that lies beside his brother's body.
He places the enormous sack on his back and departs.

Froh's outstretched hand points to the bridge, their route to Valhalla.

Froh:
Zur Burg führt die Brücke,
leicht doch fest eurem Fuß:
beschreitet kühn ihren schrecklosen Pfad!

Froh: *(to the Gods)*
The bridge leads you to he fortress,
its path firm beneath your feet:
tread undaunted on its terrorless path!

Wotan:
Abendlich strahlt der Sonne Auge;
in prächtiger Gluth prangt glänzend die Burg.
In des Morgens Scheine muthig schimmernd,
lag sie herrenlos, hehr verlockend vor mir.
Von Morgen bis Abend, in Müh' und Angst,
nicht wonnig ward sie gewonnen! Es naht die
Nacht: vor ihrem Neid biete sie Bergung nun.

So grüß' ich die Burg,
sicher vor Bang' und Grau'n!

Folge mir, Frau: in Walhall wohne mit mir!

Wotan: *(contemplating the sight)*
In the twilight, the fortress shines in
splendor.
In the morning, it will proudly glisten and
beckon me to share its glory.
From morning until evening, I toiled toward
its fulfllment, now as night nears
I long for the shelter it offers me.

I salute the fortress, that will shelter me
from anxiety and despair!
(turning to Fricka)
Follow me, wife! Dwell with me in Valhalla!

Fricka:
Was deutet der Name?
Nie, dünkt mich, hört' ich ihn nennen.

Fricka:
What does the name mean?
Strangely, I never heard it before.

Wotan:
Was, mächtig der Furcht mein Muth mir erfand
wenn siegend es lebt, leg' es den Sinn dir dar!

Wotan:
My courage taught me to master fear.
My triumphs will make the meaning clearer.

Wotan takes Fricka by the hand, and accompanies her toward the bridge:
Froh, Freia and Donner follow. Loge remains, looking contemptuosly after the Gods.

Loge:
Ihrem Ende eilen sie zu,
die so stark in Bestehen sich wähnen.
Fast schäm' ich mich mit ihnen zu schaffen;
zur leckenden Lohe mich wieder zu

Loge:
They hasten to their end, even though they
believe themselves to be indestructable.
I am ashamed to share in their dealings;
I feel myself yearning to wander amid the

wandeln, spür' ich lockende Lust:
sie aufzuzehren, die einst mich gezähmt,
statt mit den Blinden blöd zu vergeh'n,
und wären es göttlichste Götter!
nicht dumm dünkte mich das!
Bedenken will ich's: wer weiß, was ich thu'!

flickering flames,
and burn those who once bound me,
rather than foolishly
join in the Gods' destruction.
I must think of my future;
who knows what will happen?

Loge assumes an apathetic demeanor, with respect to joining with the Gods.
As the Rhinemaidens are heard lamenting their Gold, Wotan stops to listen to them.

Rheintöchter:
Rheingold! Rheingold! Reines Gold!
Wie lauter und hell leuchtest hold du uns!

Rhine Daughters: *(in the valley below)*
Rhinegold! Rhinegold! Guileless Gold!
Pure Gold, bright and clear!

Wotan:
Welch' Klagen dringt zu mir her?

Wotan:
What are those mournful sounds?

Rheintöchter:
Um dich, du klares, wir nun klagen:

Rhine Daughters:
We lament your luster.

Loge:
Des Rheines Kinder beklagen des Goldes
Raub.

Loge:
The Rhine daughters lament their stolen
Gold.

Rheintöchter:
Gebt uns das Gold! Gebt uns das Gold!

Rhine Daughters:
Return the Gold to us! Return the Gold!

Wotan:
Verwünschte Nicker!

Wotan:
Accursed nixies!

Rheintöchter:
O gebt uns das reine zurück!

Rhine Daughters:
Return our passed glory again!

Wotan:
Wehre ihrem Geneck's!

Wotan:
Quiet their accursed noise!

Loge:
Ihr da im Wasser! was weint ihr herauf?
Hört, was Wotan euch wünscht!
Glänzt nicht mehr euch Mädchen das Gold,
in der Götter neuem Glanze sonn't euch
selig fortan!

Loge: *(calling down toward the valley)*
You, in the river, why wail to us?
Hear what Wotan will do!
Your Gold shall gleam no more.
Henceforth, bask in the bliss of the Gods'
new radiance!

Rheintöchter:
Rheingold! Rheingold! Reines Gold!
O leuchtete noch in der Tiefe dein laut'rer
Tand!

Rhine Daughters:
Rhinegold! Rhinegold! Guileless gold!
If only the treasure was back here, glittering
again!

Traulich und treu ist's nur in der Tiefe: Those above, who revel in its glory, are
falsch und feig ist was dort oben sich freut!   false; its honor only resides in these depths!

The Gods cross the bridge to Valhalla, their new fortress.

END of DAS RHEINGOLD

DICTIONARY OF OPERA AND MUSICAL TERMS

Accelerando - Play the music faster, but gradually.

Adagio - At a slow or gliding tempo, not as slow as largo, but not as fast as andante.

Agitato - Restless or agitated.

Allegro - At a brisk or lively tempo, faster than andante but not as fast as presto.

Andante - A moderately slow, easy-going tempo.

Appoggiatura - An extra or embellishing note preceding a main melodic note. Usually written as a note of smaller size, it shares the time value of the main note.

Arabesque - Flourishes or fancy patterns usually applying to vocal virtuosity.

Aria - A solo song usually structured in a formal pattern. Arias generally convey reflective and introspective thoughts rather than descriptive action.

Arietta - A shortened form of aria.

Arioso - A musical passage or composition having a mixture of free recitative and metrical song.

Arpeggio - Producing the tones of a chord in succession rather than simultaneously.

Atonal - Music that is not anchored in traditional musical tonality; it does not use the diatonic scale and has no keynote or tonal center.

Ballad opera - Eighteenth-century English opera consisting of spoken dialogue and music derived from popular ballad and folksong sources. The most famous is *The Beggar's Opera,* which is a satire of the Italian opera seria.

Bar - A vertical line across the stave that divides the music into measures.

Baritone - A male singing voice ranging between bass and tenor.

Baroque - A style of artistic expression prevalent in the 17th century that is marked by the use of complex forms, bold ornamentation, and florid decoration. The Baroque period extends from approximately 1600 to 1750 and includes the works of the original creators of modern opera, the Camerata, as well as the later works by Bach and Handel.

Bass - The lowest male voice, usually divided into categories such as:

> **Basso buffo** - A bass voice that specializes in comic roles: Dr. Bartolo in Rossini's *The Barber of Seville.*

> **Basso cantante** - A bass voice that demonstrates melodic singing quality: King Philip in Verdi's *Don Carlos.*

> **Basso profundo** - the deepest, most profound, or most dramatic of bass voices: Sarastro in Mozart's *The Magic Flute*.

Bel canto - Literally, "beautiful singing." It originated in Italian opera of the 17th and 18th centuries and stressed beautiful tones produced with ease, clarity, purity, and evenness, together with an agile vocal technique and virtuosity. Bel canto flourished in the first half of the 19th century in the works of Rossini, Bellini, and Donizetti.

Cabaletta - A lively, concluding portion of an aria or duet. The term is derived from the Italian word "cavallo," or horse: it metaphorically describes a horse galloping to the finish line.

Cadenza - A flourish or brilliant part of an aria (or concerto) commonly inserted just before a finale. It is usually performed without accompaniment.

Camerata - A gathering of Florentine writers and musicians between 1590 and 1600 who attempted to recreate what they believed was the ancient Greek theatrical synthesis of drama, music, and stage spectacle; their experimentation led to the creation of the early structural forms of modern opera.

Cantabile - An indication that the singer should sing sweetly.

Cantata - A choral piece generally containing Scriptural narrative texts: the *St. Matthew Passion* of Bach.

Cantilena - Literally, "little song." A lyrical melody meant to be played or sung "cantabile," or with sweetness and expression.

Canzone - A short, lyrical operatic song usually containing no narrative association with the drama but rather simply reflecting the character's state of mind: Cherubino's "Voi che sapete" in Mozart's *The Marriage of Figaro.*

Castrato - A young male singer who was surgically castrated to retain his treble voice.

Cavatina - A short aria popular in 18th and 19th century opera that usually heralded the entrance of a principal singer.

Classical Period - A period roughly between the Baroque and Romantic periods, the late 18th through the early 19th centuries. Stylistically, the music of the period stresses clarity, precision, and rigid structural forms.

Coda - A trailer added on by the composer after the music's natural conclusion. The coda serves as a formal closing to the piece.

Coloratura - Literally, "colored": it refers to a soprano singing in the bel canto tradition. It is a singing technique that requires great agility, virtuosity, embellishments and ornamentation: The Queen of the Night's aria, "Zum Leiden bin ich auserkoren," from Mozart's *The Magic Flute*.

Commedia dell'arte - A popular form of dramatic presentation originating in Renaissance Italy in which highly stylized characters were involved in comic plots involving mistaken identities and misunderstandings. Two of the standard characters were Harlequin and Colombine: The "play within a play" in Leoncavallo's *I Pagliacci*.

Comprimario - A singer who performs secondary character roles such as confidantes, servants, and messengers.

Continuo, Basso continuo - A bass part (as for a keyboard or stringed instrument) that was used especially in baroque ensemble music; it consists of an independent succession of bass notes that indicate the required chords and their appropriate harmonies. Also called *figured bass, thoroughbass*.

Contralto - The lowest female voice, derived from "contra" against, and "alto" voice; a voice between the tenor and mezzo-soprano.

Countertenor - A high male voice generally singing within the female high soprano ranges.

Counterpoint - The combination of two or more independent melodies into a single harmonic texture in which each retains its linear character. The most sophisticated form of counterpoint is the fugue form, in which from two to six melodies can be used; the voices are combined, each providing a variation on the basic theme but each retaining its relation to the whole.

Crescendo - A gradual increase in the volume of a musical passage.

Da capo - Literally, "from the top"; repeat. Early 17th-century da capo arias were in the form of A B A, with the second A section repeating the first, but with ornamentation.

Deus ex machina - Literally "god out of a machine." A dramatic technique in which a person or thing appears or is introduced suddenly and unexpectedly; it provides a contrived solution to an apparently insoluble dramatic difficulty.

Diatonic - A major or minor musical scale that comprises intervals of five whole steps and two half steps.

Diminuendo - Gradually becoming softer; the opposite of crescendo.

Dissonance - A mingling of discordant sounds that do not harmonize within the diatonic scale.

Diva - Literally, "goddess"; generally the term refers to a leading female opera star who either possesses, or pretends to possess, great rank.

Dominant - The fifth tone of the diatonic scale; in the key of C, the dominant is G.

Dramatic soprano or tenor - A voice that is powerful, possesses endurance, and is generally projected in a declamatory style.

Dramma giocoso - Literally, "amusing (or humorous) drama." An opera whose story combines both serious and comic elements: Mozart's *Don Giovanni*.

Falsetto - A lighter or "false" voice; an artificially-produced high singing voice that extends above the range of the full voice.

Fioritura - It., "flowering"; a flowering ornamentation or embellishment of the vocal line within an aria.

Forte, fortissimo - Forte (*f*) means loud; mezzo forte (*mf*) is fairly loud; fortissimo (*ff*) is even louder; additional *fff*'s indicate greater degrees of loudness.

Glissando - Literally, "gliding." A rapid sliding up or down the scale.

Grand opera - An opera in which there is no spoken dialogue and the entire text is set to music, frequently treating serious and tragic subjects. Grand opera flourished in France in the 19th century (Meyerbeer); the genre is epic in scale and combines spectacle, large choruses, scenery, and huge orchestras.

Heldentenor - A tenor with a powerful dramatic voice who possesses brilliant top notes and vocal stamina. Heldentenors are well suited to heroic (Wagnerian) roles: Lauritz Melchior in Wagner's *Tristan und Isolde.*

Imbroglio - Literally, "intrigue"; an operatic scene portraying chaos and confusion, with appropriate diverse melodies and rhythms.

Largo or larghetto - Largo indicates a very slow tempo, broad and with dignity. Larghetto is at a slightly faster tempo than largo.

Legato - Literally, "tied" or "bound"; successive tones that are connected smoothly. The opposite of legato is staccato (short and plucked tones.)

Leitmotif - Literally, "leading motive." A musical fragment characterizing a person, thing, feeling, or idea that provides associations when it recurs.

Libretto - Literally, "little book"; the text of an opera.

Lied - A German song; the plural is "lieder." Originally, a German art song of the late 18th century.

Lyric - A voice that is light and delicate.

Maestro - From the Italian "master"; a term of respect to conductors, composers, directors, and great musicians.

Melodrama - Words spoken over music. Melodrama appears in Beethoven's *Fidelio* and flourished during the late 19th century in the operas of Massenet (*Manon* and *Werther*).

Mezza voce - Literally, "medium voice"; singing with medium or half volume. It is sometimes intended as a vocal means to intensify emotion.

Mezzo-soprano - A woman's voice with a range between soprano and contralto.

Obbligato - An accompaniment to a solo or principal melody that is usually played by an important, single instrument.

Octave - A musical interval embracing eight diatonic degrees; from C to C is an octave.

Opera - Literally, "work"; a dramatic or comic play in which music is the primary vehicle that conveys its story.

Opera buffa - Italian comic opera that flourished during the bel canto era. Highlighting the opera buffa genre were buffo characters who were usually basses singing patter songs: Dr. Bartolo in Rossini's *The Barber of Seville*; Dr. Dulcamara in Donizetti's *The Elixir of Love.*

Opéra comique - A French opera characterized by spoken dialogue interspersed between the musical numbers, as opposed to grand opera in which there is no spoken dialogue. Opéra comique subjects can be either comic or tragic.

Operetta, or light opera - Operas that contain comic elements and generally a light romantic plot: Strauss's *Die Fledermaus*, Offenbach's *La Périchole*, and Lehar's *The Merry Widow.* In operettas, there is usually much spoken dialogue, dancing, practical jokes, and mistaken identities.

Oratorio - A lengthy choral work, usually of a religious nature and consisting chiefly of recitatives, arias, and choruses, but performed without action or scenery: Handel's *Messiah.*

Ornamentation - Extra embellishing notes—appoggiaturas, trills, roulades, or cadenzas—that enhance a melodic line.

Overture - The orchestral introduction to a musical dramatic work that sometimes incorporates musical themes within the work. Overtures are instrumental pieces that are generally performed independently of their respective operas in concert.

Parlando - Literally, "speaking"; the imitation of speech while singing, or singing that is almost speaking over the music. Parlando sections are usually short and have minimal orchestral accompaniment.

Patter song - A song with words that are rapidly and quickly delivered. Figaro's "Largo al factotum" in Rossini's *The Barber of Seville* is a patter song.

Pentatonic - A five-note scale. Pentatonic music is most prevalent in Far Eastern countries.

Piano - A performance indication for soft volume.

Pitch - The property of a musical tone that is determined by the frequency of the waves producing it.

Pizzicato - An indication that notes are to be played by plucking the strings instead of stroking the string with the bow.

Polyphony - Literally, "many voices." A style of musical composition in which two or more independent melodies are juxtaposed; counterpoint.

Polytonal - Several tonal schemes used simultaneously.

Portamento - A continuous gliding movement from one tone to another through all the intervening pitches.

Prelude - An orchestral introduction to an act or a whole opera that precedes the opening scene.

Presto, prestissimo - Vigorous, and with the utmost speed.

Prima donna - Literally, "first lady." The female star or principal singer in an opera cast or opera company.

Prologue - A piece sung before the curtain goes up on the opera proper: Tonio's Prologue in Leoncavallo's *I Pagliacci.*

Quaver - An eighth note.

Range - The span of tonal pitch of a particular voice: soprano, mezzo-soprano, contralto, tenor, baritone, and bass.

Recitative - A formal device used to advance the plot. It is usually sung in a rhythmically free vocal style that imitates the natural inflections of speech; it conveys the dialogue and narrative in operas and oratorios. *Secco*, or dry, recitative is accompanied by harpsichord and sometimes with other continuo instruments; *accompagnato* indicates that the recitative is accompanied by the orchestra.

Ritornello - A refrain, or short recurrent instrumental passage between elements of a vocal composition.

Romanza - A solo song that is usually sentimental; it is shorter and less complex than an aria and rarely deals with terror, rage, or anger.

Romantic Period - The Romantic period is usually considered to be between the early 19th and early 20th centuries. Romanticists found inspiration in nature and man. Von Weber's *Der Freischütz* and Beethoven's *Fidelio* (1805) are considered the first German Romantic operas; many of Verdi's operas as well as the early operas of Wagner are also considered Romantic operas.

Roulade - A florid, embellished melody sung to one syllable.

Rubato - An expressive technique, literally meaning "robbed"; it is a fluctuation of tempo within a musical phrase, often against a rhythmically steady accompaniment.

Secco - "Dry"; the type of accompaniment for recitative played by the harpsichord and sometimes continuo instruments.

Semitone - A half step, the smallest distance between two notes. In the key of C, the half steps are from E to F and from B to C.

Serial music - Music based on a series of tones in a chosen pattern without regard for traditional tonality.

Sforzando - Sudden loudness and force; it must stand out from the texture and be emphasized by an accent.

Singspiel - Literally, "song drama." Early German style of opera employing spoken dialogue between songs: Mozart's *The Magic Flute.*

Soprano - The highest range of the female voice ranging from lyric (light and graceful quality) to dramatic (fuller and heavier in tone).

Sotto voce - Literally, "below the voice"; sung softly between a whisper and a quiet conversational tone.

Soubrette - A soprano who sings supporting roles in comic opera: Adele in Strauss's *Die Fledermaus*; Despina in Mozart's *Così fan tutte.*

Spinto - From the Italian "spingere" (to push); a singer with lyric vocal qualities who "pushes" the voice to achieve heavier dramatic qualities.

Sprechstimme - Literally, "speaking voice." The singer half sings a note and half speaks; the declamation sounds like speaking but the duration of pitch makes it seem almost like singing.

Staccato - Short, clipped, detached, rapid articulation; the opposite of legato.

Stretto - Literally, "narrow." A concluding passage performed in a quick tempo to create a musical climax.

Strophe - Strophe is a rhythmic system of repeating lines. A musical setting of a strophic text is characterized by the repetition of the same music for all strophes.

Syncopation - A shifting of the beat forward or back from its usual place in the bar; a temporary displacement of the regular metrical accent in music caused typically by stressing the weak beat.

Supernumerary - A "super"; a performer with a non-singing and non-speaking role: "Spear-carrier."

Symphonic poem - A large orchestral work in one continuous movement, usually narrative or descriptive in character: Franz Liszt's *Les Preludes*; Richard Strauss's *Don Juan, Till Eulenspiegel,* and *Ein Heldenleben.*

Tempo - The speed at which music is performed.

Tenor - The highest natural male voice.

Tessitura - The usual range of a voice part.

Tonality - The organization of all the tones and harmonies of a piece of music in relation to a tonic (the first tone of its scale).

Tone poem - An orchestral piece with a program.

Tonic - The principal tone of the key in which a piece is written. C is the tonic of C major.

Trill - Two adjacent notes rapidly and repeatedly alternated.

Tutti - All together.

Twelve-tone - The twelve chromatic tones of the octave placed in a chosen fixed order and constituting, with some permitted permutations and derivations, the melodic and harmonic material of a serial musical piece. Each note of the chromatic scale is used as part of the melody before any other note is repeated.

Verismo - Literally "truth"; the artistic use of contemporary everyday material in preference to the heroic or legendary in opera. A movement particularly in Italian opera during the late 19th and early 20th centuries: Mascagni's *Cavalleria rusticana*.

Vibrato - A "vibration"; a slightly tremulous effect imparted to vocal or instrumental tone to enrich and intensify sound, and add warmth and expressiveness through slight and rapid variations in pitch.

Opera Journeys™ Mini Guide Series

Opera Journeys™ Libretto Series

Opera Classics Library™ Series

A History of Opera: Milestones and Metamorphoses

Puccini Companion: the Glorious Dozen

Mozart's da Ponte Operas

Fifty Timeless Opera Classics

PUCCINI COMPANION: THE GLORIOUS DOZEN

756-page Soft Cover volume
Each Puccini Chapter features:

COMPLETE LIBRETTO
Italian-English side-by-side

STORY NARRATIVE
with 100s of Music Highlight Examples

ANALYSIS AND COMMENTARY

Print or Ebook

A HISTORY of OPERA: MILESTONES and METAMORPHOSES

432 pages, soft cover / 21 chapters
featuring   **Over 250 music examples**
• A comprehensive survey of milestones in opera history
• All periods are analyzed in depth:
Baroque, Classical, Romantic, Bel Canto, Opera Buffa, German
Romanticism, Wagner and music drama, Verismo,
plus analyses of the "Tristan Chord," atonalism, minimalism...

Print or Ebook

OPERA JOURNEYS' COLLECTION: FIFTY TIMELESS OPERA CLASSICS

816-page Soft Cover volume

Print or EBook

A collection of fifty·of the most popular operas
in the Opera Journeys Mini Guide Series,
each with Story Narrative and 100s of Music Examples,
PLUS insightful,in delpth commentary and analysis

MOZART'S DA PONTE OPERAS:

Don Giovanni, The Marriage of Figaro, Così fan tutte
348-page Soft or Hard Cover Edition
Print or Ebook
Mozart: Master of Musical Characterization;
Da Ponte: Ambassador of Italian Culture.
Featuring: Principal Characters, Brief Story Synopsis, Story Narrative, Music
Highlight Examples, and insightful in depth Commentary and Analysis, PLUS
a newly translated LIBRETTO of each opera
with Italian/English translation side-by-side.

ORDER: Opera Journeys' Web Site www.operajourneys.com

OPERA JOURNEYS LIBRETTO SERIES

Print or Ebook

New translations (side-by-side) with Music Highlight Examples

•Aida •The Barber of Seville •La Bohème
•Carmen •Cavalleria Rusticana •La Cenerentola
•Così fan tutte •Don Carlo •Don Giovanni
•La Fanciulla del West •Gianni Schicchi
•Lucia di Lammermoor •Madama Butterfly
•The Magic Flute •Manon Lescaut
•The Marriage of Figaro •A Masked Ball
•Otello •I Pagliacci •Rigoletto •La Rondine
•Salome Samson and Delilah •Suor Angelica
•Il Tabarro •Tosca •La Traviata •Il Trovatore •Turandot

OPERA JOURNEYS MINI GUIDE SERIES

Print or Ebook

featuring 125 titles

• *Brief Story Synopsis*

• *Principal Characters*

• *Story Narrative*

• *Music Highlight Examples*

• *Commentary and Analysis*

•The Abduction from the Seraglio •Adriana Lecouvreur •L'Africaine •Aida •Andrea Chénier
•Anna Bolena •Ariadne auf Naxos •Armida •Attila •The Ballad of Baby Doe •The Barber of Seville
•Duke Bluebeard's Castle •La Bohème •Boris Godunov •Candide •Capriccio •Carmen
•Cavalleria Rusticana •Cendrillon •La Cenerentola •La Clemenza di Tito •Le Comte Ory
•Così fan tutte •The Crucible •La Damnation de Faust •The Death of Klinghoffer •Doctor Atomic
• Don Carlo • Don Giovanni •Don Pasquale •La Donna del Lago •The Elixir of Love •Elektra •Ernani
•Eugene Onegin •Falstaff •La Fanciulla del West •Faust •La Fille du Régiment
•Fidelio •Die Fledermaus •The Flying Dutchman •Die Frau ohne Schatten
•Der Freischütz •Gianni Schicchi •La Gioconda •Hamlet •Hansel and Gretel •Henry VIII
•Iolanta •L'Italiana in Algeri •Les Huguenots •Iphigénie en Tauride •Julius Caesar •Lakmé
•Lohengrin •Lucia di Lammermoor •Macbeth •Madama Butterfly •The Magic Flute
•The Makropolis Case •Manon •Manon Lescaut •Maria Stuarda •The Marriage of Figaro
•A Masked Ball •Die Meistersinger •The Mikado •Nabucco •Nixon in China •Norma
•Of Mice and Men •Orfeo ed Euridice •Otello •I Pagliacci •Parsifal •The Pearl Fishers
•Pelléas et Mélisande •Porgy and Bess •Prince Igor •I Puritani •The Queen of Spades
•The Rake's Progress •The Rape of Lucretia •The Rhinegold •Rigoletto •The Ring of the Nibelung
•Roberto Devereaux •Rodalinda •Roméo et Juliette •La Rondine •Der Rosenkavalier •Rusalka
•Salome •Samson and Delilah •Show Boat •Siegfried •Simon Boccanegra •La Sonnambula
•Suor Angelica •Susannah •Il Tabarro •The Tales of Hoffmann •Tannhäuser •Thaïs •Tosca
•La Traviata •Tristan and Isolde •Il Trittico •Les Troyens •Il Trovatore •Turandot
•Twilight of the Gods •The Valkyrie •Werther •West Side Story •Wozzeck

ORDER: Opera Journeys' Web Site www.operajourneys.com

Opera Journeys Publishing

at the vanguard of opera education

OPERA CLASSICS LIBRARY™

OPERA STUDY GUIDES and LIBRETTOS

EXCLUSIVE SALE at the Kindle Store and Amazon
Over 40 titles - available in Ebook and/or PRINT

Aida	*The Elixir of Love*	*The Magic Flute*	*The Ring of the*
The Barber of Seville	*d'Amore Ernani*	*Manon Lescaut*	*Nibelung La Rondine*
La Boheme	*La Fanciulla del West*	*The Marriage of Figaro*	*Salome*
Don Carlo	*Gianni Schicchi*	*A Masked Ball*	*Samson and Delilah*
Carmen	*Don Giovanni*	*Nabucco*	*Suor Angelica*
Cavalleria Rusticana	*Lucia di Lammermoor*	*Norma*	*Il Tabarro*
La Cenerentola	*Luisa Miller*	*Otello*	*Tosca*
Cosi fan tutte	*Macbeth*	*I Pagliacci*	*La Traviata*
La Donna del Lago	*Madama Butterfly*	*Rigoletto*	*Il Trovatore*
			Turandot

Featuring
Principal Characters
Brief Story Synopsis

Featuring
Story Narrative
with Music Examples

Featuring
Libretto
Translation side-by-side

Made in United States
Orlando, FL
29 March 2023

31524562R00068